Late Show Fun Facts

By David Letterman

and the *Late Show* Writers:

Eric Stangel	Justin Stangel
Bill Scheft	Steve Young
Tom Ruprecht	Lee Ellenberg
Jeremy Weiner	Joe Grossman
Bob Borden	Rob Burnett

HYPERION

New York

Library of Congress Cataloging-in-Publication Data is available upon request.

ISBN 978-1-4013-2307-3

Hyperion books are available for special promotions, premiums, or corporate training.
For details contact Michael Rentas, Proprietary Markets,
Hyperion, 77 West 66th Street, 12th floor, New York, New York 10023,
or call 212-456-0133.

Acknowledgments

Thanks to:

Nancy Agostini

Mary Barclay

Stephanie Birkitt

Joanna DeMartin

Barbara Gaines

Jill Goodwin

Kristen Lange

Dana Marano

Michael Z. McIntee

Fred Nigro

Valerie Schaer

The *Late Show* Staff and Crew

FOREWORD FROM DAVE LETTERMAN

The questions I'm most frequently asked: "Do you play cards?" "How much did you pay for those smart-looking slacks?" "Do you know someone named Gail?" "May I borrow your bandana?" No sir, in truth, the question I get most often: "Have you ever been in prison?" This always brings a smile to my face, and more than a flood of fun memories.

In 1967, having no money, no friends, no goal, no direction, no education, no desire, no luck, I turned my life to the simple and easy enjoyment of radio. Yes! I spent my days and nights listening to a radio I had stolen from an appliance store downtown. What a hold-up. And believe me, the prices those marrow-sucking parasites were charging... They had it coming. Check this out: $29.95 for some lousy foreign transistor job built by, I don't know, monkeys? Children? Childish monkeys? Who knows? But take it from me, it was junk.

I hope you know me well enough to know that by nature, I don't go around stealing. Although talk to CBS about my paycheck! Yikes! But seriously, 30 clams for a box that overheats and hums? Did somebody say "sounds like my honeymoon?" Thank you! Anyway, you get where I'm coming from on this deal.

So one day I'm lucky enough to get a signal strong enough to identify feral grunts, and I hear some lard-ass yakking about a contest jerks like me could call in and win a giant wad of cash. Here's the deal: The radio station plays a list of songs cut into little bits. Name all the songs, and you're King For a Day.

FOREWORD FROM DAVE LETTERMAN

Yeah, but what you don't know, songs in little bits is no day at Wal-Mart. You'd have to be Beethoven or some genius like that. Maybe Einstein or Edison. Maybe not, all those guys were deaf. Right?

So now I realize if I want a shot at winning the contest I gotta get some help. I knew my parents—and I love them both to the point of nearly unnatural feelings—were going to be of no help. Dad would never admit it, but things like the radio give him the heebie-jeebies. Not in the usual way, but like creep-city-from-outer-space-kind-of-way heebie-jeebies. "If we all listen to the radio as much as you, what do you think ears will look like in 100 years?" "Anyone's guess, Dad," I thought. Mom, well-meaning, always on Dad's side, and most days full of painkillers, choking sobs, dropping to her knees and loudly barking, "Help, help, oh Jesus, Jesus, Jesus help." Not much help there.

I did toy with the idea of asking our neighbor, a foul-smelling widower named Buddy, for help. Ever since his wife Tina died (one day she just popped), Buddy listened to the radio 24/7. Often falling asleep in his own stench while his radio blared to high hell. If I'm entirely honest about it, Buddy could have helped me, I guess. In the same way two people consume more oxygen than one. Does that make sense? Well, guess what—I never solved the radio musical contest for losers. I only knew two of the songs. Some piece of crap by Brenda Lee, or Connie Francis, and an opus by a guy named Ferlin Husky. Can you imagine? "We are the Husky family; let's name our boy Ferlin." Oh, brother!

I called in anyway, thinking I might bust up the deal for everybody, which in a way is winning. The grand prize was one thousand four hundred and thirty dollars (AM 1430). Wow!! A lot of dough, even today. Yes, don't kid yourselves, that's cash I could have used. Candy, cigarettes, a new car for Mom, a fully equipped woodworking shop for Dad. Some kind of atomic personal hovering scooter device for me. Well guess what? No such luck. All I got for calling the station was a lousy Faron Young record. Get this: he was talking to his house. "Hello Walls." Nice song!!

Buddy, our foul-smelling neighbor, was discovered dead and all bloated in his basement. Lord knows how long he'd been down there. He stuck a fork in a toaster and fat-boy went poof!!! Busybody neighbors who crawled through the basement window found Buddy, said the place didn't smell much worse than when the foul-smelling Buddy was alive.

After about six months on the market, a couple named Roger and Lynn Driscoll bought Buddy's house. They yanked the carpet, roach-bombed the cellar, put a sissy-looking birdbath in the front yard, flipped the house, and made a nasty seven grand. The new owners, Charles and Billie Garrison, moved right in. No clue that the foul-smelling Buddy had turned himself inside out in their rec room. But, believe you me, there were many times I was tempted to let them in on Buddy's secret. Like when they called the cops on Dad the night he came home loaded and took a leak in their birdbath.

I have never been in prison.

Thanks for watching. Enjoy the book.

Dave Letterman

Dear Reader,

I was 17 years old when I encountered my first Fun Fact: "Edward R. Murrow smoked in his sleep." The experience proved to be a life-changing event.

I'd grown up in modest circumstances, part of a family that had little interest in facts, fun or otherwise. But when I graduated from West Tipton Indiana Community College in 1970 with a degree in Miscellaneous Studies, I knew the FBMI was where I belonged. As I rose through the ranks from junior researcher to director, I worked to transform the bureau from a sleepy civil service backwater to the dynamic organization it is today. With over 20,000 staffers, an annual budget in excess of a billion dollars, and a yearly Fun Fact output approaching the one-million mark, the FBMI touches the daily life of almost every American, as well as many Canadians.

Truly, this is a golden age of miscellaneous information. As director of the FBMI, I take great pleasure in bringing you this book, but this is only the beginning. Currently in the works are Fun Fact feature films, video games, ringtones, pay-per-view specials, action figures, a line of bottled water, temporary tattoos, face paint, free balloons for the kids, and much, much more. Keep checking in at www.fbmi.gov for the latest!

Of course, I want to extend a special thanks to David Letterman, who has been an unwavering supporter of the FBMI and its mission since we met at my friend Paul Shaffer's wedding a number of years ago. This book would not have happened without Dave's enthusiastic inclusion of Fun Facts on his popular "Last Night Show."

Finally, I wish to dedicate this book to the hardworking men and women of the FBMI, to the American people, to David Letterman, and to a lesser extent Paul Shaffer.

And now, enjoy the book. I guarantee it'll be fun— and that's a fact!

Gary Sherman, director,
Federal Bureau of Miscellaneous Information

FBMI DISCLAIMER

The Federal Bureau of Miscellaneous Information makes no warranty, either express or implied, as to the entertainment value or veracity of the "Fun Facts" presented herein. While every attempt has been made by the FBMI to identify and delete any statements that represent outright falsehood or are deemed likely to cause sadness or melancholy, both "fun" and "truth" are highly subjective topics. The consumer therefore agrees to indemnify and hold harmless the FBMI and its employees and affiliates, as well as all other federal agencies and their employees and affiliates, in the event of a Fun Fact failing to impart correct information or pleasurable delight. I, the FBMI's chief legal counsel, am so confident that nobody reads these long disclaimers that I'm inserting the phrase "grab-ass." Furthermore, in the event of a dispute regarding the entertainment value or factual nature of a Fun Fact statement, any lawsuit or legal action against the FBMI and/or its employees will be governed by the articles of the 1959 Antwerp Infotainment Convention, which state in part that "no person or persons claiming damage from the lack of reality or amusement or grab-ass in an infotainment-related assertion shall have legal standing to pursue redress except via the World Court of Infotainment Law, which shall convene no less than every three years in Antwerp or a comparable Low Country municipality." People think lawyers aren't fun, but we're really a crazy bunch. You should see how we cut loose at the annual FBMI legal department holiday party. For example, there's quite a lot of grab-ass. Wow, I did it again! Being a lawyer is hilarious. Not really. Most days I want to kill myself. For any further questions concerning your legal rights pertaining to Fun Facts and international infotainment law, consult those subhuman puds at Jacoby & Meyers.

LATE SHOW FUN FACTS

One in every three Americans loses an eye in an umbrella accident.

If your name is Todd, it might as well be Scott.

If your name is Scott, it might as well be Todd.

It takes 15 chickens to make six McDonald's Chicken McNuggets.

At any given moment in the United States, there's someone eating toffee-covered peanuts.

One in every 2,000 babies is born fully clothed.

Currently there is only one living American named Maxine.

The old saying, "Calories don't count on your birthday," has been scientifically proven.

Seventy-eight percent of Canadian high school students drop out each year.

Nancy Reagan is responsible for coining the phrase "Are you yanking my chain?"

Enough hairpieces are sold in the United States each year to cover Neptune.

Buzz Aldrin is the only person ever to have taken a leak on the moon.

The Old Testament contains 22 references to brownies being "sinfully delicious."

Wyoming, the country's least-populated state, is home to just six people.

Einstein estimated that his Theory of Relativity got him laid more than a hundred times.

During a three-year lucky streak from 1956 to 1959, no one in America died.

Sixty-four percent of all coin tosses land on "heads."

The average time on the eastern seaboard is 4:30 P.M.

There is no legal difference between a "dining set" and a "dinette set."

The average male thinks about Joan Collins nine times every hour.

No one named Gary has ever been pope.

If you see the glass as half full, you're an optimist. If you see it through lenses you prescribed for yourself, you're an optometrist.

The first bowling ball was just called a ball.

Thomas Edison never received credit for inventing the flat-front chino, although he did.

The biggest American fear is public speaking. The second is accidentally ingesting raw lamb.

Those who knew him say Benito Mussolini did an amazing Porky Pig impression.

The Broadway show *Rent* closed after the theater's landlord evicted them.

LATE SHOW FUN FACTS

The United States' border with Mexico is over 2,000 miles long but only six inches wide.

The equator is so long, it could circle the Earth once.

At least two Alamo Rent A Car locations are managed by descendants of Davy Crockett.

Columbia University offers 20 percent off medical school tuition to students who bring their own cadavers.

After bingo, the second most popular recreational activity at senior centers is leg wrestling.

The highest-rated television show of all time was the *Facts of Life* episode where Tootie gets new roller skates.

Geronimo was conceived while his parents were skydiving.

The 1952 Summer Olympics were canceled due to a high pollen count.

The record for Academy Award nominations is 14, shared by *Titanic* and *Meatballs Part II*.

The most popular tourist destination in the world: the Bay of Fundy.

Orson Welles was buried alive.

Montana is the only state where horseplay is illegal.

Walt Whitman's dying words were "kiss my ass."

The first present ever to be gift wrapped was a bicycle horn.

In 1788, Benjamin Franklin published the world's first erotic almanac.

Every year, surgeons leave an average of five cell phones inside patients.

Ninety-six percent of wrong numbers involve a guy saying, "Larry?"

In ancient Egypt, a man's wealth was determined by the length of his tongue.

Mae West and Adolf Hitler had the same driving instructor.

There is no word in the English language that rhymes with "zoocumber."

Crepe paper has no purpose or use.

Candy cigarettes are just as harmful as real cigarettes.

Scientists who've been studying pigeons say they're definitely up to something.

In the late 1920s, the Periodic Table of Elements briefly included paprika.

In Denmark, it is illegal for two members of the same family to own the same shirt.

In Westchester County, New York, there is a barber named Tony DeBarber.

A significant majority of birthday wishes involve lesbians.

Radio-industry researchers have found that office productivity doubles on "Two-for-Tuesdays."

Most Americans wish they had more than one rake.

Three percent of American income is spent on onions.

The first material used in breast implants was cookie dough.

The record for most appearances on the cover of *Time* magazine, 26, is held by Tom Arnold.

At any given moment, 20 million American men don't realize their fly is down.

There is no function that Dr. Joyce Brothers will not attend.

Seventy-five percent of fishermen say they'd rather not be fishing.

The fastest animal in the world is the chicken.

Napoleon's last word was "squat."

The llama is the only animal that saunters.

There's never been a Jewish person named Vince.

After years of smoking, Frosty the Snowman died from corncob lung.

Fidel Castro came up with a sexual position called the "Cuban Sandwich."

LATE SHOW FUN FACTS

Before the invention of the touch-tone phone, 900 Americans died each year in rotary-dialing accidents.

The polar bear has no natural enemies, nor does it have any friends.

The book most frequently stolen from public libraries: the autobiography of Fran Tarkenton.

Despite years of trial and error, Thomas Edison could never perfect a five-blade razor.

Aztec emperor Montezuma's most trusted warriors were permitted to call him "Monty."

Two of Jesus's 12 apostles were temps.

Benjamin Franklin coined the term "funbags."

A Freedom of Information Act request was recently filed for the government to reveal the location of the Hidden Valley Ranch.

The invention that later became Silly Putty was originally intended as a contraceptive device.

Scientists at Bell Labs have now identified nearly 70 ways to leave your lover.

Mamie Eisenhower liked it rough.

LATE SHOW FUN FACTS

For one week in 1920, the United States Postal Service accepted bacon and other smoked meats taped to the corner of an envelope as postage.

The Dalai Lama has an extensive souvenir shot glass collection.

Global warming is worse on Tuesdays.

Before the advent of dental records, corpses were identified by jazz records.

Medicine-bottle child safety caps are also hard to open for short adults.

Christopher Weldon of Columbus, Ohio, is the only person ever to actually laugh all the way to the bank.

In Alaska, the dessert known as "baked Alaska" is called "baked here."

Prior to 1936, elevators only went up, not down.

Though it remains open, no one has visited Epcot Center in 12 years.

The King of Queens is loosely based on the relationship between Adolf Hitler and Eva Braun.

While they're still not allowed to drive cars, as of May 2006, Saudi Arabian women may operate riding mowers.

LATE SHOW FUN FACTS

During a screening of Neil Simon's *The Goodbye Girl* at the Vatican, someone asked Pope Paul VI to remove his hat.

Authorities cannot say for certain whether Jim Nabors is dead or alive.

Due to global warming, by 2050, the average temperature of gazpacho will have risen two degrees.

When held by a person who is more than seven feet tall, a ladle is just called a "spoon."

Moses's last name was Weintraub.

After centuries of weak sales, bumper stickers skyrocketed in popularity with the invention of the automobile.

Newton's Fourth Law states: "No fat chicks."

135	E	1
90	F P	2
75	T O Z	3
60	M O E D	4
45	E R N E U	5
30	N E U K E R	6
22	F L I K K E R O P	7
15	S M E E R L A P	8
10	E T C L E P B Z E	9
6	D P L T E E P E R F L T E	10

The most common form of elevator small talk involves discussing the size of a coworker's ass.

The standard American eye chart contains several Dutch obscenities.

Not only did Lincoln have a secretary named Kennedy, he also nailed her.

No one has ever written to a cooking show to request a recipe.

Bill Gates has paid tens of millions of dollars to have his childhood bullies tracked down and killed.

LATE SHOW FUN FACTS

In his or her lifetime, the average American will swallow at least one pair of dice.

The concept of "soup of the day" was invented by the Aztecs.

The longest yard ever measured was three feet two inches.

Before the *Titanic* sank, nine passengers had already died from tainted lox.

George Foreman has been on three juries, but has never been foreman.

The average Midtown Manhattan window washer witnesses quite a lot of sexual activity.

Gandhi kept a trampoline in his office.

When Americans are asked to name their favorite food on a cob, nearly 60 percent reply "corn."

While it's true Will Rogers said, "I never met a man I didn't like," he never met David Schwimmer.

The apple that hit Isaac Newton on the head was actually thrown by some neighborhood punks.

During his later fireside chats, Franklin Roosevelt would invite listeners to phone in and play Lesbian Dating Game.

In addition to the "eye for an eye, tooth for a tooth" philosophy, Hammurabi's Code clearly stated "bros before hos."

At the Last Supper, five apostles ordered dessert.

In addition to his famous violins, Stradivarius also made salad tongs.

Warren Buffett made his billions betting on jai alai.

At his inauguration, Eisenhower was chewing gum.

Because he thought it was funny, President George W. Bush signed his first piece of legislation as "Evel Knievel."

The original set of *Hollywood Squares* was modeled after a Danish prison.

Scientists believe that by 2012, we will run out of "signs that you might be a redneck."

Winston Churchill's British accent was fake.

During his time as a lawyer, Abraham Lincoln briefly ran his legal practice out of a bowling alley.

When the first Crayola crayons were introduced in 1903, the only colors were brown and dark brown.

In the first modern Olympics in 1896, the gold medal-winning high jump was two feet eight inches.

Since 9/11, airport screeners are allowed to try on passengers' pants.

LATE SHOW FUN FACTS

Because of the dangers of smoking, the surgeon general has advised circus clowns to switch from exploding cigars to exploding gum.

Prostitution notwithstanding, historians believe the world's oldest profession is landscaping.

Former White House cleaning lady Mildred Herman is the only woman to have had sex with both John F. Kennedy and Bill Clinton.

Match Game host Gene Rayburn's headstone reads "loving father, friend, and blank."

Thirteen years after *Cheers* went off the air, cast member John Ratzenberger continues to act out new episodes in his garage.

Genghis Khan was the only Mongol ever to have been bar mitzvahed.

The most popular lock combination is Jamie Farr's birthday, 7–1–34.

Genetic engineers say they will soon have the technology to create a person who is part Baldwin brother and part Wayans brother.

Seventy-one percent of paramedics admit to having shocked someone with a defibrillator for fun.

When the Americans invaded Iraq in 2003, Saddam Hussein was watching *The Rockford Files*.

While the sun is hot, it's nowhere near as hot as people would have you believe.

FBMI TIMELINE

1920 The 19th Amendment gives women the right to submit Fun Facts.

1933 In his first fireside chat, President Roosevelt uses a Fun Fact as an icebreaker: "Until 1880, potatoes were used mostly for pranks."

1876 First use of the term "Fun Facts," in an FBMI booklet distributed at Philadelphia's Centennial Exposition. Companion "Serious Facts" fail to catch on and are discontinued.

1860 The FBMI launches the Pony Express in order to speed the transport of miscellaneous information to California.

| 1850 | 1860 | 1870 | 1880 | 1890 | 1900 | 1910 | 1920 | 1930 |

1857 President James Buchanan, disturbed that so much information doesn't fit into major categories, creates the Federal Bureau of Miscellaneous Information.

1886 Statue of Liberty dedicated; as a gesture of France's admiration for Fun Facts, the tablet Liberty is holding reads "FBMI" (changed in the 1930s to "July 4, 1776").

1901 President McKinley is fatally shot by a disgruntled former FBMI researcher.

1863 The FBMI supplies President Lincoln with an "entertaining truth" included in an early draft of the Gettysburg Address: "Confederate General Robert E. Lee has swallowed over two dozen brass buttons chewed from his uniform jacket."

1930 Due to the Depression, the FBMI is forced to lay off the entire Geology and Particulate Matter departments.

1986 Director Gary Sherman and the FBMI play the Harlem Globetrotters on the Great Wall of China.

1959 The FBMI begins production of Fun Facts in color.

1968 First Fun Fact sent into space aboard Apollo 8: "Technically, the watermelon is a nut."

1943 The FBMI ramps up wartime production 200 percent, sending over 180,000 Fun Facts to American GIs overseas.

2007 O.J. Simpson bursts into the FBMI offices brandishing a gun in order to retrieve all "Juice"-related Fun Facts.

| 1940 | 1950 | 1960 | 1970 | 1980 | 1990 | 2000 | 2010 |

1962 Rare Fun Fact brings record $1.2 million at auction; a typographical error had resulted in the printing of a Swedish obscenity.

1984 At the height of "Fun Facts Mania," director Gary Sherman makes a cameo appearance on *Miami Vice* as a smuggler importing illegal facts from Colombia.

1998 In one week during the height of the Clinton impeachment, the FBMI receives over 11,000 letters from guys claiming credit for the phrase "oral sex is not sex."

1936 At the Berlin Olympics, Hitler is enraged when the FBMI's Fun Facts are funnier and more factual than those from the Nazis' Behörde Verschiedener Informationen.

1953 In the bureau's darkest hour, FBMI staffers Julius and Ethel Rosenberg are executed for passing Fun Facts to the Soviet Union.

1976 Gala opening of the Fun Facts Gentlemen's Club.

In response to complaints, Campbell's has removed the letter "F" from their alphabet soup.

Scientists project that by 2040, global warming will mean the end of Carvel ice cream cakes.

Twenty-three percent of Americans believe that Columbus's landing in the New World was faked.

Contrary to conventional wisdom, surgeons say the second or third cut is usually the deepest.

Until a 1960 Supreme Court ruling, the artificial sweetener Equal was called Separate but Equal.

Instead of turning into a superhero, most people bitten by a radioactive spider just develop a minor rash.

No one has actually bought anything from Radio Shack in close to a year.

Scientific studies now reveal many similarities between apples and oranges.

"Al Jazeera" is an Arabic term meaning "the jazeera."

Houdini's first escape in 1891 was from a snug-fitting sweater-vest.

Vice President Dick Cheney became wealthy after wisely investing his winnings from *Tic-Tac-Dough.*

When the situation gets difficult, the difficult get situation.

LATE SHOW FUN FACTS

Seventy-seven percent of people who say "yes" to fresh-ground pepper at a restaurant really don't want it.

The founder of the USDA is buried in a tomb at the base of the food pyramid.

Fewer than three percent of blues songs are about how well things are going.

Alex Rodriguez earns close to 40,000 dollars per at-bat, which he receives in cash while in the on-deck circle.

One wing of the Pentagon is a Macy's.

In addition to many unfinished works of art, Pablo Picasso left behind an unfinished basement.

To compensate for their lack of sight, blind people have developed an acute sense of humor.

Despite historians' claims, it can now be confirmed that the Renaissance was not all it was cracked up to be.

Hearses carrying a body are eligible to drive in the carpool lane.

While no man is an island, it is believed that no one has come closer than Dom DeLuise.

Mr. Peanut recently switched from a monocle to a single contact lens.

Although he hates America, Osama bin Laden has always wanted to visit Dollywood.

Conspiracy theorists believe that I Can't Believe It's Not Butter is indeed butter.

Early is the new late.

The favorite rock band of 61 percent of electricians is AC/DC.

By a 20–to–1 margin, maple syrup outsells oak syrup.

The first microwave ovens rotated the food but didn't cook it.

The surgeon general never smokes, except when he's drinking.

The average Amish person spends nearly three minutes a year in traffic.

By law, a doctor may not use a tongue depressor to depress other parts of your body.

Hawaiian tailors use weed whackers to shorten grass skirts.

There are three retired admirals on the board of Old Navy.

Archie Bunker's chair is in the Smithsonian Institution's Museum of American History because on the show, the Bunkers lived in the Smithsonian.

If it's your birthday, most airlines will let you exit the plane via the inflatable slide.

LATE SHOW FUN FACTS

Matthew is the only gospel that mentions Jesus being ticklish.

During the 1970s, the Nobel Committee handed out an award for Best R&B or Funk Album.

Major League Baseball rules dictate that each season the Minnesota Twins' roster include one set of twins.

In 2002, Poland Spring had to recall four million bottles that contained H_3O.

Ancient Inca drawings of the sun closely resemble what people today call "Pac-Man."

Nancy Sinatra's biggest hit was inspired by the instructions that came with a pair of boots.

Assassin Sirhan Sirhan's middle name: Rick.

The last time Bono wasn't wearing sunglasses was during a 1998 shower.

Due to its shoddy human-rights record, North Korea is not allowed to be a member nation of the International House of Pancakes.

In 1971, comedian Henny Youngman sank into a deep depression when someone finally did take his wife.

At some point in his or her life, one out of four Americans will be attacked by a rabid squirrel.

Charles Manson and Dick Van Patten were college roommates.

Over 15,000 people were killed during the cola wars of the 1980s.

Although Americans take credit for the first moon landing, the Vikings are believed to have preceded them by 600 years.

Scientists have found a link between a midsummer spike in birth rates and wives who wore slutty costumes the previous Halloween.

Due to wartime fabric shortages, from 1943 to 1945, American males were forced to walk around pantsless.

Contrary to the popular slogan, 68 percent of what happens in Vegas leads to divorce and/or bankruptcy.

In 1956, the man who played Smokey the Bear accidentally set fire to a Woolworth's department store.

Not many women named Lydia are considered hot.

If there's a fire at Willy Wonka's chocolate factory, workers must evacuate via the stairs, not the Wonkavator.

The Vatican currently employs six stunt-popes.

In his will, kitchen-gadget inventor Ron Popeil has asked that his remains be julienned.

Only six percent of people who "shake and rattle" also "roll."

Sixty-eight percent of loafer wearers say if money weren't an issue, they'd upgrade to tasseled loafers.

In addition to its versatile knives, the Swiss Army is known for its multifunctional pants.

Even the Colorado Rockies manager could only name about three guys on the team.

The movie *The Bridges of Madison County* got a thumbs-up from the American Society of Civil Engineers.

For a brief period during the 1970s, the penny was modified to give Abraham Lincoln a Dorothy Hamill-like haircut.

After bringing the Ten Commandments down from Mount Sinai, Moses was repeatedly asked why number 1 was the least funny.

In addition to its billions of hamburgers sold over the years, McDonald's has sold nearly two dozen salads.

The refrigerator, the microwave, and the Slurpee machine were all invented by fat guys.

Eleanor Roosevelt ran Washington, DC's first escort service.

The Wright brothers' cousin Duane invented the luggage carousel.

The first poll ever taken revealed 95 percent of those asked could do without custard.

Thirty-seven of the 42 men elected to serve as president of the United States at one time worked as mall Santas.

Richard Simmons has been pepper-sprayed over 50 times.

The term "jack-of-all-trades" was named after the multitalented actor Jack Lord.

The real reason President Nixon resigned: shoplifting.

Mikhail Gorbachev decided America can't be all bad after seeing Phoebe Cates in *Fast Times at Ridgemont High.*

If you press Shift-Control-F5 on a Windows-equipped computer, you'll see an explicit video of Bill Gates's wedding night.

The so-called Spanish-American War of 1898 was actually more Italy and Japan.

In 1983, baseball Hall of Famer George Brett was ejected from a game for wearing argyle socks.

There is no Eskimo word for becoming dizzy on a spiral staircase.

Kellogg's recently signed a deal with the Vatican to sell Pope-Tarts.

LATE SHOW FUN FACTS

The wardrobe for Vladimir Lenin's preserved body was provided by Botany 500.

George Clooney recently joined match.com to try to meet women.

A baby has over ten different cries for strained lentils.

Ugandan dictator Idi Amin never forgot a birthday.

You need a combined SAT score of at least 1150 to get into the Crips.

Twenty-five percent of barbers have carpets woven from hair clippings in their homes.

During the 20th century, Western Union did a brisk business in X-rated telegrams.

Because of global warming, next year the NHL will shrink to eight teams.

For 25 dollars, New York City will name a pothole after you.

Most popular wedding present: CO_2 fire extinguisher.

To delay their executions by 24 hours, savvy death-row inmates order Peking duck for their final meal.

Seven *Hollywood Squares* panelists were seriously injured when Dom DeLuise, Louie Anderson, and Roseanne Barr were all seated in the top row.

FBM
FAQ

FBMI FAQ

Q: "What does FBMI stand for?"
A: Federal Bureau of Miscellaneous Information.

Q: "Who is in charge of the FBMI?"
A: The director of the FBMI is Gary Sherman.

Q: "What does FAQ stand for?"
A: Frequently Asked Questions.

Q: "What are the FBMI's hours of operation?"
A: The FBMI is open Monday through Friday from 9A.M. to 5P.M. Please note: The FBMI is closed on all national holidays and Gary Sherman's birthday.

Q: "Where can I find a shareholder report on the FBMI's financial standings?"
A: You seem to have us confused with Firstbank Corporation (NYSE: FBMI). As a government agency, the FBMI is not publicly traded but believe us, we wish we had Firstbank's kind of money!

FBMI FAQ

Q: "I found a factual error in a Fun Fact. How do I report it?"

A: You'd be the first! In the history of the FBMI, we've never had to make a retraction, but if you're just looking to make trouble, write to quality control supervisor Doug Perry at dperry@fbmi.gov.

Q: "Does Gary Sherman write Fun Facts on his own?"

A: No. Gary is lucky enough to have a team of writers who generate most of the material, but not a single Fun Fact makes it out to you, the customer, without Gary's personal approval.

Q: "Why aren't Fun Facts as much fun as they were when I was a kid?"

A: There are always a few critics who say that Fun Facts peaked in the 1950s, 1960s, 1970s, or whenever, but market research shows that Fun Facts are being enjoyed by more people* than at any time in the FBMI's history. But you're probably right.

*in key demographics men aged 18–34 and women aged 18–49

Q: "I remember reading a Fun Facts collection that was filled with coarse language. Why would you publish such a thing?"

A: Unfortunately, there are many cheap imitators of Fun Facts, some of which resort to profanity for shock value (i.e. "Phun Phax"). But official FBMI Fun Facts are always wholesome and family-friendly—that's our promise to you.

Q: "I heard Gary Sherman was the best man at bandleader Paul Shaffer's wedding. Would he consider being my best man, too?"

A: Yes.

Q: "If I send you a photo of the pus-leaking lesions I have developed on my lower torso, could you diagnose them?"

A: While knowledgeable in most matters, our staff is not qualified to make medical diagnoses. However, we would be able to tell you what is "fun" and a "fact" about this or any other medical problem.

FBMI FAQ

Q: "Are the FBMI and the FBI related?"

A: No. However, sometimes we accidentally get evidence that's supposed to be delivered to the FBI, such as carpet fibers, blood samples, and terror tips. We throw that stuff away.

Q: "Director Sherman, like millions of other American women, I'm spellbound by your rugged good looks and your worldly, sophisticated demeanor. Are you single?"

A: It's kind of complicated. Call me at my office.

Q: "Where is the FBMI director in the presidential order of succession?"

A: The FBMI director is seventh in line, after the secretary of defense but ahead of the attorney general. In 1881, FBMI director Chester A. Arthur became president after James Garfield and several other top government officials died in a ballooning mishap.

Q: "I'm new to Fun Facts. What do I need to know before I dive in?"

A: Safety first! On average, more than 55 people die each year from Fun Fact–related causes.

Q: "Is the FBMI part of the secret-world government run by the Freemasons and the Trilateral Commission?"

A: No. You're thinking of OSHA.

Q: "What is the atomic weight of praseodymium?"

A: Praseodymium's atomic weight is 140.90765.

Q: "Are all recipes submitted to the Pillsbury Bake-Off read and judged, or are just some of the recipes selected for review?"

A: All entries in the Pillsbury Bake-Off that meet the entry requirements are read and judged by home economists from the official judging agency. From the many entries, the best are selected for kitchen testing and evaluation by taste panels. Most entrants describe themselves as lonely.

FBMI FAQ

Q: "What does FBMI director Gary Sherman look like without a shirt?"

A: A young Danny Aiello. It's kind of complicated. Call me at my office.

Q: "Are tours of the FBMI office available for classes?"

A: Yes. The first step is to contact Ms. Marilyn Szerencsy in our public relations department. The second step is to apologize to your class for not going someplace cool, like Wayne Newton's Ranch and Equestrian Center.

Q: "Has the FBMI ever been sued?"

A: Yes, by the M. K. Gandhi Institute for Nonviolence, after a Fun Fact was published stating the spiritual leader would often break his fast with tacos.

Q: "How much would you charge to write a Fun Fact about a friend or relative of mine as a gift for a special occasion?"

A: If you have to ask, you can't afford it.

Q: "Has anyone ever made a movie about the FBMI?"

A: No, but you may recall the short-lived ABC television series
Mr. Miscellaneous (1994), starring Robert Wagner as the fictional
Barry Sherman.

Q: "How does the FBMI ensure all of its information is miscellaneous?"

A: Everything is cross-referenced multiple times with the Federal Bureau of
Specific Information.

Q: "Of all the Fun Facts, is there one that is considered the most fun?"

A: The FBMI does not disclose that information. But here's a hint: It has something to do with bacon.

Q: "Is there anything you want to ask me?"

A: Um, no; I'm good.

At Phil Rizzuto's funeral, the hearse left the service early to beat traffic.

Don Ho spent six years in jail for beating a tourist to death with a tiki torch.

On two separate occasions, Gandhi broke his fast with tacos.

The 50 stars on the United States flag stand for the 50 ways to leave your lover.

As brilliant as Albert Einstein was, he could never talk Mrs. Einstein into a three-way.

Pat Sajak has spent millions trying to develop a letter that would be a vowel/consonant hybrid.

Few ranchers actually use ranch dressing.

Blueberry is the most commonly shoplifted muffin.

Pit bulls can smell fear—and pie.

The original proposal for daylight saving time also called for "hump day" to be moved to Thursday.

During a sugar shortage in the 1940s, many Americans flavored their coffee with bouillon cubes.

Due to his size, President William Howard Taft was buried in a swimming pool.

The word "apple" comes from the Latin word meaning "apple."

Half-and-Half is usually closer to 60/40.

Thanks to a sophisticated robot developed by Japanese inventors, it now only takes one to tango.

Prior to the passage of the Nineteenth Amendment in 1920, women were not allowed to press elevator buttons.

Ancient Egyptians are credited with inventing the "lost and found" box.

In February 1981, the Dalai Lama won 14,000 dollars on *Card Sharks.*

The film *Snakes on a Plane* is very loosely based on a novel by Jane Austen.

Because of shortages caused by the war, in 1942, triple-decker sandwiches were made with two slices of bread.

Zsa Zsa Gabor has no memory of husbands three and five.

The most exclusive country clubs in America admit neither women nor men.

A cucumber is 96 percent water and four percent cucumber.

Other than nuclear weaponry, the only difference between North and South Korea is that South Korea uses the DH.

Al Roker couldn't care less what it's like in your neck of the woods.

LATE SHOW FUN FACTS

The Native American who cried in the classic anti-pollution commercial also cried in a commercial for Dentyne.

Major League Baseball contends the only thing keeping Pete Rose out of the Hall of Fame is his soup-bowl haircut.

Widely distributed in 1588, the world's first piece of junk mail was an advertisement for erotic wigs.

Tony Bennett also left an umbrella stand in San Francisco.

In the original *The Wizard of Oz* screenplay, the Tin Man was looking for a tin whore.

The inventor of TiVo named his son "StiVo."

Prior to 1981, FCC regulations prohibited the use of the word "walnuts" on radio or television.

Medical experts say if Elvis hadn't died of heart failure on August 16, 1977, he probably would have died of heart failure on August 23, 1977.

Springfield, Massachusetts, is home to both the Basketball Hall of Fame and the Basket Hall of Fame.

The earliest binoculars made things look as close as they actually were.

The television show *Lassie* ran for 140 years in dog-years.

Although the United States population is supposedly 300 million, the government admits that figure may include several thousand houseplants.

At the end of his life, Thomas Edison didn't have enough money to pay his electric bill.

Only 13 percent of all nitro-burning cars are funny.

James Garner works five days a week at a Malibu, California, Denny's.

Apple has spent nearly 200 million dollars trying to develop a wooden iPod for the Amish.

If the 2008 election were held today, Howie Mandel would be elected president.

Loni Anderson and Louie Anderson often get each other's mail.

To try and give aliens a sense of who we are, NASA beams episodes of *Who's the Boss?* into space.

Katharine Hepburn's last words were, "Read me some more of those 'you might be a redneck' jokes."

The first entry ever to be searched on Google was "lesbian wrestling."

If a doctor leaves an object in you during surgery, it legally becomes your property.

Socrates was the first person to ask why we drive on a parkway and park on a driveway.

Wink Martindale has a brother named Blink.

After "Hello", the most popular telephone greeting is, "'Sup, bitch?"

The original Lassie had rabies and was destroyed.

Before the advent of self-adhesive stamps, postage was responsible for 83 percent of America's licking.

In the days before limousines, people flaunted their wealth by riding very long horses.

In 1979, Pope John Paul II declared the microwave oven a miracle.

Until 1970, the United States Census Bureau kept track of people who looked "shifty."

The frozen head of Ted Williams wears a wool cap.

According to complaints from his wife, elevator pioneer Elisha Otis refused to go down.

To boost interest in coin collecting, in 1976, the Treasury briefly replaced the phrase "In God We Trust" with "Dy-no-mite!"

The original recipe for Animal Crackers called for each cracker to be made from the meat of the corresponding animal.

Theologians now believe the Last Supper may have been more of a brunch.

People magazine's Sexiest Man Alive is seventh in line to the presidency.

In 1976, the Kentucky Derby was won by a couple of fraternity guys in a horse costume.

Dr. Robert Jarvik invented the world's first artificial heart out of an empty beer can and a corncob pipe.

James Madison wrote Article One, Section Five of the Constitution while naked.

It's a poorly kept secret in the pharmaceutical industry that Colgate toothpaste is just mint-flavored cream cheese.

Fortune cookies are the world's only clairvoyant snack.

Due to a clerical error, the Nobel Prize in Chemistry was once awarded to a parakeet.

The person Americans would least like to have dinner with is Gerry Cooney.

Woodrow Wilson's eldest daughter was named Whoopi.

Merv Griffin briefly produced a game show in the mid-60s called *You Can Kiss My Ass.*

LATE SHOW FUN FACTS

Applebee's is so named because its founder was stung to death by bees while eating an apple.

In 2004, the FBI foiled an Al Qaeda plot to disrupt the cattle judging at the Illinois state fair.

Robert E. Lee's middle name was Ernie.

Despite the name, most gravy boats are not seaworthy.

The first sandwich consisted of a slice of bread with another slice on the bottom and a third on top.

No one has ever TiVo'd *According to Jim*.

NASA included the moon buggy on the Apollo 15 mission to see if it was possible to "peel out" on the moon.

Eva Braun's parents felt she could do much better than Hitler.

Because of an onion allergy, the singer Meat Loaf can't eat meat loaf.

The ancient Egyptians originated the concept, "You break it, you buy it."

In Oregon, it's illegal to transport someone in a wheelbarrow for money.

In 1926, stainless steel replaced the much less popular "stained steel."

Burt Bacharach ends every concert by flipping over his piano.

A study revealed that the technological innovation people would find most impressive is a robot that makes pancakes.

LATE SHOW FUN FACTS

Before a budget cut, the Lincoln Memorial's chair was supposed to come with a matching ottoman.

Researchers at Sara Lee have spent nearly three billion dollars trying to find a way for people to have their cake and eat it too.

Depending on context, the Hawaiian word "aloha" can mean "hello," "good-bye," "love," or "gravy."

The Center for Sleep Research has spent seven million dollars trying to disprove the widely held belief that if you snooze, you lose.

FUN FACTS ABOUT THE FBMI

FUN FACTS ABOUT THE FBMI

A rare edition of Fun Facts published with the misprint "FBNI" was sold by Sotheby's for 15,000 dollars.

In addition to its Washington, DC, offices, the FBMI maintains a climate-controlled vault in rural Virginia where backup copies of every Fun Fact ever written are stored.

In 1965, Tommy Thorson, an FBMI mailroom worker who played in a rock band in his spare time, hit No. 92 on the Billboard Chart with the novelty song "F-B-M-I Love You So."

The mascot for the FBMI's softball team: Facty the Pelican.

Richard Nixon is the only president ever to veto a Fun Fact (the Fun Fact in question: "Unbeknownst to his wife, Pat, Richard Nixon taped their wedding night").

In the first draft of *Mr. Smith Goes to Washington*, instead of being elected to the senate, Jimmy Stewart's character becomes associate director of the FBMI.

FBMI office coordinator Joyce Berman is easy.

In Utah, it's illegal for unwed couples to read Fun Facts to one another.

During the 1979 takeover of the U.S. Embassy in Iran, embassy personnel frantically shredded dozens of pages of Fun Facts.

FUN FACTS ABOUT THE FBMI

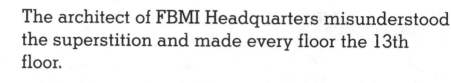

The architect of FBMI Headquarters misunderstood the superstition and made every floor the 13th floor.

Much like the president, the FBMI director is always accompanied by an NSA agent with a briefcase handcuffed to his wrist—although it's filled with cookies.

The building in Appomattox, Virginia, in which General Lee surrendered to General Grant to end the Civil War was an FBMI satellite office.

FBMI Headquarters is built over an ancient Indian burial ground.

The FBMI's annual holiday party is awkward and sad.

During the 1960 presidential race, then-Senator John F. Kennedy called for a massive increase in the FBMI's budget to close the "miscellaneous information gap" with the Soviet Union.

It costs taxpayers 1.2 million dollars a year to equip FBMI toilets with urinal pucks emblazoned with the departmental logo.

Twelve percent of FBMI staffers write Fun Facts without wearing pants.

Because he is the subject of so many Fun Facts, a movement is under way to rename FBMI Headquarters "The Jim Belushi Building of Miscellaneous Information."

FUN FACTS ABOUT THE FBMI

FBMI merchandise is sewn by underpaid Peruvian children in the building's crawl space.

The FBMI has a strict "no cursing" policy. Staffers are encouraged to say "frak" like they do on *Battlestar Galactica.*

Each year, several thousand couples get engaged in front of FBMI Headquarters.

The FBMI has stopped importing Fun Facts from China because the Fun Facts were found to contain unacceptable levels of lead.

In 2002, the FBMI switched from Wite-Out to Liquid Paper.

The most popular item in the FBMI break room vending machine: Andy Capp's Hot Fries.

Since 2000, 11 FBMI staffers have failed paternity tests on *Maury*.

The FBMI is the only U.S. government agency to have been predicted by Nostradamus.

When Franklin Roosevelt read Fun Facts to the nation over the radio, Eleanor Roosevelt used to walk into the room naked to make him laugh.

Because of a sponsorship deal with Marlboro, from 1951 to 1953, all Fun Facts had to be about cigarettes.

FUN FACTS ABOUT THE FBMI

The Dutch wear wooden underpants.

After saying "One small step," Neil Armstrong recited some of his favorite Fun Facts from the surface of the moon.

The Wright brothers invented the airplane as a means of quickly delivering Fun Facts to a distant relative.

"Mean Joe" Greene was originally supposed to film a commercial in which he tossed an envelope of Fun Facts to a young fan; unfortunately, he had already signed a deal with Coke.

If you took all the Fun Facts the FBMI has published and laid them end-to-end, they would circle the globe (twice, if you used a larger font).

Elvis was reading Fun Facts when he died in the bathroom.

The United States makes up five percent of the world's population, yet consumes nearly 80 percent of the world's Fun Facts.

In 1989, Gary Sherman became the only man to be named both *Time*'s Man of the Year and *People*'s Sexiest Man Alive.

Golf ball-sized hail can be used in any PGA-sanctioned event.

The shoelace was invented before the shoe.

At the first Thanksgiving, Squanto introduced the pilgrims to green bean casserole with cream of mushroom soup and crispy onion rings.

Because "Jeb" stands for "John Ellis Bush," when people say, "Jeb Bush," they're actually saying "John Ellis Bush Bush."

Originally, answers on *Jeopardy!* were given in the form of a threat.

No one has a birthday on March 16th.

Despite Mother Teresa's charitable spirit, when trick-or-treaters came around, she turned off the lights and pretended not to be home.

Since the release of *The Bucket List,* bucket sales have quadrupled.

In the history of divorce settlements, no wife has ever asked for her husband's shot glass collection.

Historians believe Amelia Earhart's final flight got lost because her navigator, like most men, wouldn't ask for directions.

By 2015, 7-Elevens will be upgraded to 8-Twelves.

LATE SHOW FUN FACTS

Although a lobster's claw is strong enough to crack a walnut, lobsters don't care for walnuts.

Robert Frost didn't like poetry, but he wrote it because he knew it would get him laid.

In 1977, Costa Rica applied to become one of the Benelux countries, but was rejected.

Sixty-four percent of American students cannot find Funkytown on a map.

Although he won the election, Herbert Hoover's promise of "a chicken in every pot" cost him the chicken vote.

The United States Department of Commerce does nothing.

Before the invention of popcorn, moviegoers would snack on entire cobs of corn.

Due to a typographical error, Ohio law mandates a three-day waiting period before you can buy gum.

The most common liquid confiscated by airport security is honey mustard.

While filming *The Wizard of Oz*, scarecrow actor Ray Bolger constantly complained of chigger-laden straw playing hell with his nuts.

LATE SHOW FUN FACTS

Researchers trying to figure out what happened to the dinosaurs now suspect there may have been foul play.

When the world's fattest dwarf died, he was buried in a Casio keyboard box.

For a donation, the CDC will name a disease after you.

A team of Caltech scientists determined that in 72 percent of cases, you can judge a book by its cover.

The manufacturer of Q-tips warns they should not be used for any purpose whatsoever.

Nancy Reagan can palm a basketball.

Despite the name, the vast majority of Good Humor men are miserable sons of bitches.

Twenty-two percent of grooms secretly try on their bride's wedding gown.

Saddam Hussein sent out invitations to his hanging.

Our tallest president: Wilt Chamberlain.

Thomas Jefferson went by the nickname "TJ Jazzy Jeff."

The nickel is only 25 percent nickel; the dime is only 15 percent dime.

LATE SHOW FUN FACTS

Mel Gibson once reluctantly admitted that he enjoys Hebrew National hot dogs.

George Washington actually crossed the Delaware twice because the first time he forgot his big hat.

Orville Wright left his wife after she screamed "Wilbur" during sex.

Due to a horse shortage, the 1936 Kentucky Derby was run with giraffes.

In the wake of a 1992 violation, New York State revoked the Beastie Boys' "license to ill."

Ironically, the show *American Bandstand* used a bandstand that was built in Canada.

Bud Selig says Barry Bonds will be eligible for the Hall of Fame if he agrees to get an asterisk tattooed on his ass.

The last request of Clara Peller, the "Where's the Beef?" lady from the 1980s Wendy's commercial, was to be ground up and turned into a hamburger.

There are only three documented cases of people juggling in their sleep.

The Nobel Prize in Literature has twice been awarded to phone books.

The FDA technically classifies pancake batter as soup.

The country most recently admitted to the United Nations is responsible for refreshments.

LATE SHOW FUN FACTS

Tiger Woods can't play miniature golf to save his life.

In the Soviet Union, television watches you.

The most popular flavor of ChapStick is bacon.

Apple is developing an artificial heart that holds a thousand songs.

Five percent of people who have voices in their heads say at least one sounds like sportscasting legend Chick Hearn.

Albert Einstein's proudest achievement: He once bowled a 230.

Donald Trump wears twice as much makeup as his wife.

Before a family squabble, one of America's largest companies was known as Johnson & Johnson & Johnson.

Last year was the first time the queen of England knighted a guy named "Corey."

Elizabeth Taylor once divorced a man she never married.

Like George W. Bush, Saddam Hussein was a cheerleader in college.

In 1978, a man found two snowflakes that were exactly alike, but they melted in the *Real People* greenroom.

It is customary to tip tollbooth operators.

The most common street name in America is 138th Street.

The French Dip is consistently voted the world's dampest sandwich.

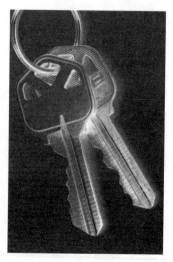

After you die, your tongue continues to grow.

The most commonly misspelled word in the English language is "Toyotathon."

George Washington never told a lie except when Martha caught him opening the neighbor's mail.

More people accidentally swallow their house keys than you would imagine.

During the studio's golden age, 16 crew members were mauled to death by the MGM lion.

On Orville Wright's second flight, he towed a banner for Coppertone.

Police lineups always put the guilty guy in the middle.

John Wayne's real name was Lydia Schiffman.

Hall-of-Fame catcher Johnny Bench sleeps in the crouching position.

Alan Shepard was the fifth astronaut to walk on the moon, but the only astronaut to leave his wallet there.

Edward R. Murrow ended his final newscast by dropping his pants and firing a rocket.

America's garbage is dumped over the Canadian border.

August 12, 1954

To whom it may concern:

While I cannot argue with your assertion that Oscar Mayer's wife divorced him because he always came home smelling like bologna, I would ask that you not trivialize my father's personal tragedies for the entertainment of others. Lord knows our family has suffered enough.

Cordially, Fritz Mayer
Chicago, Illinois

March 11, 1943
Dear FBMI:

Every Sunday, Rachele and I wake up early and read Fun Facts to each other in bed over coffee, and we're always guaranteed a smile. Keep up the good work!

Yours, Benito Mussolini
Rome, Italy

November 21, 1972

Dear Fun Facts:

Last week, you published a Fun Fact pointing out the irony that my allergies prevent me from owning a cat. Oddly enough, this never dawned on me. I'm still chuckling!

Best, Cat Stevens
London, England

LETTERS TO THE FBMI

April 27, 1996
Dear Mr. Sherman,

Last week's "Fun Facts" revealed the trade secret that police lineups always put the guilty person in the middle. I hope you're proud that you've permanently made the job of every law-enforcement worker in America more difficult. Eat shit.

Sgt. Duane Haskins, ret.
Mercer County Police Department
Burgin, Kentucky

August 3, 1975
Dear FBMI,

For most of my life, I've been very shy, uncomfortable at parties, and completely helpless around women. But after a few months of reading Fun Facts, I'm never at a loss for interesting conversation—with coworkers, strangers, or my gorgeous fiancée (even when she'd like to do more than talk!). You've changed my life forever, Fun Facts!

Thank you, Sid Phelps
Silver Spring, Maryland

Janurary 19, 1979
Dear Sirs,
Love your work. Could you please run more Fun Facts about twine?
Sincerely, Russ Albertson
Provo, Utah

June 23, 1958
To Whom It May Concern,

While it may be a fact, my six-year-old daughter found nothing "fun" about your revelation that there is no Tooth Fairy. Please cancel my subscription immediately!

Disgusted, Lois Piedmont
Elko, Nevada

February 9, 1997
Dear FBMI,

Just 24 hours ago, I was lying unconscious in the hospital following a nasty slip in the tub. The doctors didn't think I'd pull through, but then my wife sat down at my bedside and started reading some of our favorite Fun Facts out loud. I told Patty it was her voice that brought me back, but deep down, I think we both know the power of miscellaneous information.

Thank you, Doug Whitman
Purchase, New York

LETTERS TO THE FBMI

January 8, 1967
My Dear Mr. Sherman,

This is in reference to a slight inaccuracy I found in a recent "Fun Fact" regarding the Bible. "The word 'flapjacks' appears only once in the Bible." Did someone forget the Old Testament? Hello!!

Spiritually Yours,
Father Colin O'Dwyer
Boston, Massachusetts

December 18, 1985
To the FBMI,

Could you please include some Fun Facts about early 70s folk icon "Wild Bill the Mannequin Fucker?" It would mean a lot to his family. Thanks.

Wild Bill
the Mannequin Fucker Jr.
Crawfordsville, Indiana

September 22, 1999

My Good Sirs:

As the executor of Sir Laurence Olivier's estate, I take pen in hand to correct a glaring discrepancy in a recent "Fun Fact," which claimed Mr. Olivier's favorite on-screen performance was Tom Laughlin's portrayal of Billy Jack. In truth, it was his favorite performance. Period. Screen or stage.

Respectfully,

Lloyd Dunwoody

Los Angeles, California

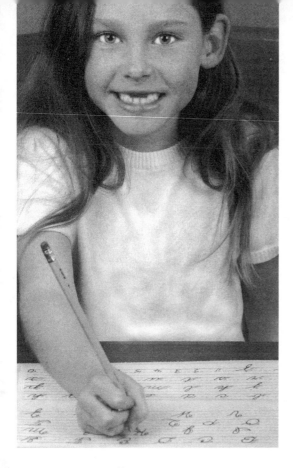

KIDS' LETTERS TO THE FBMI

KIDS' LETTERS TO THE FBMI

I like fun facts because they taught me I shouldn't lick mold.

—Tracy, age 6

I like Fun Facts because reading them is like going to school but without the mean kids who tease me about my name.

—Javier Pontoon Jr., age 7

I like Fun Facts because they give my parents something to talk about besides their grinding dislike for one another.   —Ellie, age 9

KIDS' LETTERS TO THE FBMI

I love Fun Facts because they teach you interesting things about famous people like Pope Benedict's arrest for taunting phone calls to Phil Mickelson.

—Adam, age 9

I love Fun Facts because saying "I love Fun Facts" got me out of math class to write this letter.

—Kevin, age 12

I like Fun Facts because they make me feel smarter than President Bush.

—Sarah, age 7

I love Fun Facts because
they make me laugh, like
the government's pledge
that the social security
trust fund will still be solvent
by the time I retire.

—Jill, age 11

I love Fun Facts because they
teach me about my favorite
things, like baseball and versatile
character actor Robert Loggia.

—Jay, age 8

Thank you for all the
Fun Facts. I had no
idea Rachael Ray was
a slut.

—Frankie, age 16

LATE SHOW FUN FACTS

Cloud types include cirrus, stratus, and fluffy.

In the 1970s, *Family Feud* host Richard Dawson was responsible for passing a communicable influenza that killed nearly 1,000 Americans.

Andrew Jackson was the first United States president to use a fork.

George W. Bush's cell phone ringtone is "La Cucaracha."

The FBI's eleventh most-wanted fugitive is Lyle Lovett.

Last year, 18 high-ranking chess players were disqualified for steroid use.

During World War II, Americans used an abbreviated alphabet consisting of only 18 letters.

Less than one percent of the population eats the small cup of coleslaw that comes with burgers.

Orville Wright was the first person ever to return a tray table to its upright and locked position.

In 1983, the president was given veto power over the *People's Choice Awards.*

When it was introduced in 2001, the iPod was the size of a refrigerator and held two songs.

LATE SHOW FUN FACTS

Furniture experts say you're no more likely to score on a love seat than on a regular sofa.

Walter Mondale once ended a presidential debate in 1984 by performing Jennifer Beals's *Flashdance* routine.

When a United States president dies, it is customary for his Secret Service agent to be executed and buried in an adjoining cemetery plot.

Eighty percent of museum patrons are gay.

Queen Elizabeth II only gets a ten percent discount on the *Queen Elizabeth II* cruise ship.

Wayne Gretzky prefers his soda without ice.

The earliest English muffins contained nooks, but no crannies.

The FDA has officially declared Velveeta "disgusting."

In 1991, the Federal Reserve made it a felony for your mouth to write a check your body can't cash.

The Japanese tradition of serving fish that's not cooked was invented by a very lazy chef.

The adult human heart weighs 34 pounds.

In the 1800s, atlases did not include maps of Florida because it was "too suggestive."

Porcupines are neither pine nor pork.

Before John Hancock signed the Declaration of Independence, he signed a bill in favor of alternate-side-of-the-street parking.

In the '40s, Pontiac produced a car called the Pantywaist.

Horoscopes accurately predict future events 85 percent of the time.

Planet of the Apes was loosely based on a true story.

The highest ratings in television history were recorded the night the Home Shopping Network sold Spock's ears.

Matzo ball soup is called "Jewish penicillin;" gefilte fish is known as "Jewish erythromycin."

At Brigham Young University, parties feature kegs of club soda.

Due to a clerical error, from 1931 to 1932, Delaware had a dog for governor.

After declaring bankruptcy in 1990, Donald Trump spent three years living in his car.

Fidel Castro is the only dictator ever to host *Saturday Night Live.*

During a recent trip to the DMV, Martha Stewart received license plates she made in prison.

The Q-tip was developed after serious design flaws were found in both O- and P-tips.

LATE SHOW FUN FACTS

As great as Michael Jordan was, he was never good enough to play for the Harlem Globetrotters.

Pat Sajak can't read.

David Hasselhoff pays women 30 dollars to call him "the Hoff."

Until the late 1700s, the earth actually was flat.

Larry King slept his way to the top.

Mickey Rooney once Googled himself to find out if he was still alive.

In addition to post offices and immigration offices, you can renew your passport at IHOPs.

No one named Tony has ever won a Tony Award.

Creamed corn was invented in 1955 after the great cream surplus of 1954.

Harpo Marx's production company was called Oprah Productions.

Eerie coincidences emerge if you watch *The Wizard of Oz* while listening to the *Wizard of Oz* soundtrack.

Richard Nixon would always get a laugh at family barbecues by wearing an apron that read, "I am not a cook!"

Walter Matthau smelled pretty much like he looked.

The Simon & Garfunkel song "Scarborough Fair" was about Garfunkel's secret love for WNBC anchor Chuck Scarborough.

LATE SHOW FUN FACTS

Russian President Vladimir Putin's favorite movie is
Porky's 3: Porky's Revenge.

John Madden has looked the same age since 1984.

Casey Kasem doesn't care much for music.

FedEx employees are instructed to pretend to laugh when a
customer jokes about the office looking like an airport counter.

Benjamin Franklin had a thing for fat chicks.

The most popular lifeguard gag gift is
a vibrating CPR dummy.

In 2004, former President George H.W.
Bush voted for John Kerry.

John Deere never cut a blade of grass
in his life.

The very first e-mail offered low-price Mexican tranquilizers.

For Christmas this year, Osama bin Laden gave out fleece jackets with the Al Qaeda logo.

The first telephone call Alexander Graham Bell placed was a wrong number.

After a bout with conjunctivitis, Frank Sinatra was briefly known as "Ol' Pink Eyes."

Jesus used to feel shortchanged at the holidays because his birthday fell on Christmas.

LATE SHOW FUN FACTS

George Bernard Shaw is the man who wrote the novelty greeting-card phrase, "Lordy, Lordy, You're Over Forty."

Thanks to global warming, the texture of an ice cream sandwich is right where you want it to be.

Despite the popular commercial, no one has ever said, "More Ovaltine, please."

The Civil War marked the first military use of ventriloquists.

In 1985, Hall & Oates consummated their relationship.

In Margaritaville, the leading cause of death is "wasting away."

Ninety percent of directors who cast Bill Paxton meant to hire Bill Pullman.

In 2007, Ziploc plans to introduce a body bag that seals in freshness.

The baby pictured on the Gerber label is a young William Shatner.

In 1877, Alexander Graham Bell made the first obscene phone call when he asked if Watson was wearing tight pants.

George W. Bush has never missed an episode of *Deal or No Deal.*

Confucius must've been a pain in the ass to live with.

Frank Melsky, the guy who wrote "The 12 Days of Christmas," went on to write "99 Bottles of Beer on the Wall."

Nineteen percent of Americans believe it's cruel to drop spaghetti into boiling water.

In an early draft of the Dr. Seuss classic, the green eggs and ham came with a side of home fries.

Joseph Stalin's secret to staying young was to laugh every single day.

Before the stapler was invented, everything had to fit on one page.

According to NASA rules, horseplay is prohibited on the moon.

In New Mexico, it's legal to drive while asleep.

Every casino in Las Vegas has banned legendary card counter Barbara Bush.

Following the death of Rodney Dangerfield, his widow filed a malpractice suit against Dr. Vinnie Boombatz.

Archaeologists believe Egypt's pyramids may have been built by using illegal Mexican labor.

Astronaut Deke Slayton was taken ill and had to be replaced on Apollo 8 because of bad Tang.

Before coming to power, Slobodan Milosevic hosted a radio talk show about soccer.

The seagull is the bird most likely to take a crap on your shoulder.

Tommy Lee Jones and Kim Jong Il were freshman roommates at Harvard.

Until 1922, the president and vice president shared a bed.

Twenty-two percent of Americans say that if it were legal, they'd try cannibalism.

Jonas Salk, inventor of the polio vaccine, died on a mattress in a Serta showroom.

Though she lost, Madeleine Albright once competed for breast implants on *The Howard Stern Show*.

Prior to 1900, the Chinese ate with three chopsticks.

Close friends of Iranian President Mahmoud Ahmadinejad call him "Manny."

On more than one occasion, the Rite Aid in Chappaqua, New York, has developed nude photos of Bill Clinton.

When France gave us the Statue of Liberty, they included the receipt in case we wanted to exchange it.

Neil Armstrong was also the first man on Mrs. Armstrong.

Bob Saget lives on the old set of *Full House*.

In Mexico and parts of Colombia, Starbucks coffee contains amphetamines.

The San Andreas Fault was built in the 1930s at a cost of two billion dollars.

Sheep ranchers counting the number of animals in their herd often doze off.

Two out of five airline pilots have a child named Niner.

On his deathbed, Harpo Marx honked a heartfelt good-bye to his family.

The original slogan for M&M'S candies was "Melts in your mouth, not in your pants."

Newsman Jim Lehrer is married to the woman who plays Elvira, Mistress of the Dark.

The first telephone number was 3.

Toward the end of his life, Charles Lindbergh was a flight attendant for Continental.

Though a virulent anti-Semite, Osama bin Laden has seen Woody Allen's *Annie Hall* 15 times.

The shoe Nikita Khrushchev used to bang on the United Nations table was purchased at Thom McAn.

When life hands you gators, make Gatorade.

Seventeen percent of employers say they would think less of an applicant who showed up to the job interview eating a turkey leg.

Evangelical Christians refuse to own a Dirt Devil vacuum cleaner.

A TOUR OF FBMI HEADQUARTERS

No visit to our nation's capital would be complete without a tour of FBMI Headquarters. Here's just a small sampling of the amazing things you'll see.

A TOUR OF FBMI HEADQUARTERS

The Fun Analysis Division. If it's fun, it's here!

Maybe you'll run into FBMI media relations manager Simon Kent, who coordinates Gary Sherman's appearances at state fairs and rodeos!

Located 1,200 feet below street level, this hardened bunker will allow the FBMI to continue producing Fun Facts in the event of a nuclear war or other catastrophe.

A TOUR OF FBMI HEADQUARTERS

The FBMI's oldest staffer, 102-year-old Punctuation Volunteer Herbert Green. Mr. Green adds commas to Fun Facts wherever necessary.

The FBMI cafeteria, serving what are widely considered to be the best waffles in the Washington, DC/Maryland area.

The power behind the FBMI's pneumatic tube system, which allows pages of Fun Facts to be whisked to any office in the building within 19 minutes.

A TOUR OF FBMI HEADQUARTERS

FBMI staffers let off steam at the indoor climbing wall, a 1992 gift from the grateful nation of Kuwait.

While 97 percent of Fun Facts are printed on paper, the FBMI uses this metal stamping machine to make heavy-duty Fun Facts for the military.

Lyman Floyd Rutledge, "The Father of the Fun Fact"

Marine Three, the helicopter used by Gary Sherman in the event of a miscellaneous information-related crisis.

Rutledge wrote the first Fun Fact, which stated that the favorite 18th-century prank was dipping quills in molasses.

A TOUR OF FBMI HEADQUARTERS

The FBMI East Lawn, where Jimmy Carter, Menachem Begin, and Anwar Sadat agreed to the free and open exchange of miscellaneous information among the three nations.

The Fun Fact Simulation Experience 2008! gives visitors an exhilarating, pulse-pounding, three-dimensional view of how Fun Facts are brought to life!

In an ever-increasing effort to shrink the carbon footprint of FBMI Headquarters, static electricity generated by the pneumatic tube system produces 15,000 kilowatts of electrical power, which is harnessed and used to operate the FBMI state-of-the-art chewing gum vending machine. The machine, located in the lobby, is a real favorite and offers a wide variety of popular gum. Next time you visit, treat yourself to tasty refreshment as well as a glimpse into the future.

Please don't touch! This mysterious metal hatchway has never been opened.

In 1978, a Wisconsin man was beaten by an angry mob after asking for "no cheese" on his Whopper.

To appear on *Inside the Actors Studio*, you must agree to have sex with James Lipton.

In 12 percent of the DNA tests on his program, Maury Povich is the father.

Famous composer Marvin Hamlisch spends much of his free time collecting aluminum cans.

In 1972, the FCC fined Julia Child 50,000 dollars for saying the word "nutmeat."

When he gets caught in the rain, Donald Trump smells like a basset hound.

In America, motorists drive on the right side of the road; in England, motorists drive on the left side of the road; in Norway, they drive in the middle.

The Iran-Iraq War of the 1980s was fought over whether it should be called the "Iran-Iraq" war or the "Iraq-Iran" war.

Tom Brokaw does a newscast in his living room each night for his wife.

People who live together for extended periods end up blinking at the same time.

The actual Godzilla was only seven feet tall and was killed by Japanese soldiers within minutes.

Since 1980, the runner-up in each presidential election has received a 50 dollar gift certificate to Filene's Basement.

The record high for the Northeast occurred in 1888, when temperatures in Trenton, New Jersey, reached 153 degrees.

Randy Johnson always felt Yankee pinstripes made him look tall and awkward.

Larry King wears suspenders in the shower.

During his term with the Federal Reserve, Alan Greenspan lost 2.8 billion dollars in taxpayer money betting on keno.

Alex Trebek threatens to rough up contestants if they don't give him ten percent of their winnings.

The "K" in "Kmart" stands for "Kmart."

Clint Eastwood's spaghetti Westerns doubled spaghetti sales from 1964 to 1966.

Modern Amish buggies come equipped with Sirius satellite radios.

The chicken preceded the egg by nearly three minutes.

Senator Everett Dirksen once proposed extending daylight saving time an extra hour so he'd have enough time to buy his wife an anniversary gift.

Fifty percent of Americans account for half of the United States' population.

LL Cool J once marketed a line of mail-order clothing under the name LL Cool Bean.

LATE SHOW FUN FACTS

Duran Duran got its name due to a typographical error.

According to the FAA, God is not licensed to be a copilot.

After the Taco Bell E. coli scare, "Chalupa" briefly fell out of the ten most popular baby names.

Around the world, every 23 seconds someone is having sex in a carpet store.

The eulogy at Saddam Hussein's funeral was delivered by Pat Sajak.

Candy corn outsells candy beans 200 to 1.

In the original version of Monopoly, if you landed on Ventnor Avenue and paid ten dollars, you could rent a whore.

As a young man, George W. Bush once spent three days in a revolving door.

Colonel Sanders admitted to his therapist that at age three, he was nearly pecked to death by a rooster.

When adjusted for inflation, the top-grossing movie of all time is *Police Academy 4*.

If every person in America joined hands, it would be pointless.

Oral-B is the name of a dental products company. It was also Bill Clinton's Secret Service nickname.

The Constitution guarantees every American the right to a hot meal at a fair price.

George Washington died of a wig infection.

Da Vinci's notebooks included a design for a primitive TiVo.

Originally, the Lincoln Tunnel was intended to connect Manhattan to Lincoln, Nebraska.

Due to the lengthy appeals process, Pluto won't officially be out of the solar system until at least 2010.

A winner never quilts, and a quilter never wins.

Of all grocery store employees, produce department managers have the most sex.

Anthropologists now believe that the Easter Island statues were the result of "kids fooling around."

It's hard not to be impressed when your waiter makes guacamole tableside.

Eighty-five percent of a house cat's day is spent licking something.

The first skydive was an incredibly lucky accident.

Osama bin Laden tells everyone he bowled a 300 the first time he went bowling.

President Benjamin Harrison died when he was kicked in the head by a goat.

The most popular name for a beauty salon is Curl Up and Dye.

LATE SHOW FUN FACTS

In the original DC comic, Aquaman was known as Captain Wet.

The most common name in the world is Chet.

In 1984, former New Orleans Saints head coach Bum Phillips was approved for sainthood by the Catholic Church.

Because he didn't have strong religious beliefs, Dwight Eisenhower took the oath of office on a cookbook.

If you type "Garfunkel" on Microsoft Word, the spell-checker will ask if you meant "carbuncle."

A worker loses a finger every 30 seconds at the Chef Boyardee factory.

Only two ingredients differentiate high-impact plastic from Oscar Mayer bologna.

When life hands you lemons, in addition to lemonade, you could consider making a delicious lemon meringue pie.

For the past 12 Halloweens, George W. Bush has dressed as Gilligan.

Asbestos is an excellent source of calcium.

Eddie Money is broke.

Every issue of Benjamin Franklin's popular almanac included etchings of nude, heavyset women.

Because of his expensive divorce, Paul McCartney has taken a part-time job at Quiznos.

In the first draft of *Jaws*, the creature was a moody halibut.

In 1994, Huey Lewis & the News played at Uday Hussein's 30th birthday party.

James K. Polk was America's only openly gay president.

When asked who they most admire, 54 percent of schoolchildren choose Larry Hagman.

The earliest instant oatmeal took longer to prepare than regular oatmeal.

In addition to his well-known airway obstruction maneuver, Henry Heimlich popularized several sexual positions.

The sixth leading killer in the world is chapped lips.

The average Amtrak passenger spends 14 hours a year wondering, "What's the holdup?"

Thanks to a 1971 Motown stint, Ruth Bader Ginsburg is the only person who's been a member of both the Supreme Court and the Supremes.

Every 500 feet during his historic 1953 ascent of Mount Everest, Edmund Hillary would turn to his Sherpa, Tenzing Norgay, and ask, "Are we there yet?"

The one item most Americans say they couldn't live without is the Brother P-touch Label Maker.

A FUN FACT'S JOURNEY FROM THE FBMI TO YOU

An FBMI fact generation associate arranges words in various combinations until a potential "fact" sentence is formed.

FBMI fact generation department head checks grammar, and sends copies of the sentence to the Fun Analysis Division and the Factual Verification Department.

If the Fun Quotient is determined to be at least .75, the sentence is graded "Fun OK."

Reality experts examine the sentence to see if it "feels true." A truthfulness score of 60 percent or higher is required.

Submissions judged insufficiently fun or factual are disassembled so the words can be used again, or may be donated to third-world countries.

Submissions that are both adequately factual and fun are retyped and delivered to the House of Representatives.

A FUN FACT'S JOURNEY FROM THE FBMI TO YOU

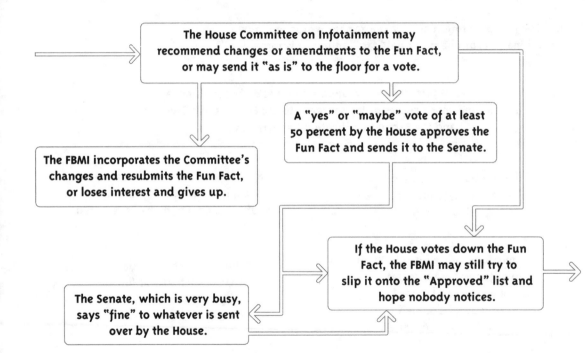

The House Committee on Infotainment may recommend changes or amendments to the Fun Fact, or may send it "as is" to the floor for a vote.

A "yes" or "maybe" vote of at least 50 percent by the House approves the Fun Fact and sends it to the Senate.

The FBMI incorporates the Committee's changes and resubmits the Fun Fact, or loses interest and gives up.

If the House votes down the Fun Fact, the FBMI may still try to slip it onto the "Approved" list and hope nobody notices.

The Senate, which is very busy, says "fine" to whatever is sent over by the House.

Approved Fun Facts are retyped and presented to the Supreme Court for review. While the court has no power to strike down Fun Facts, the Justices do enjoy leafing through them in the break room.

This box intentionally left blank.

The president signs each Fun Fact. He may, at his discretion, veto one Fun Fact which he finds unflattering or lame, per week . (Bonus Fun Fact!)

Approved Fun Facts are retyped again on acid-free archival paper, transported via armored truck to two dozen FBMI Regional Centers in the continental U.S. (Alaskan and Hawaiian Centers scheduled to open in 2011 and 2018, respectively.)

Roughly three percent of Fun Facts are lost to pilferage, vandalism, or water damage.

Several thousand Fun Facts are released each week for distribution to churches, schools, comedy-variety talk shows, and civic groups such as the Boy Scouts of America.

The Fun Fact educates and entertains you!

LATE SHOW FUN FACTS

Although they all used to live in Texas, one of George Strait's exes has since relocated to Arizona.

Jim Henson's earliest Muppets were hollowed-out animal carcasses.

Aromatherapy is just a sales gimmick to get people to buy candles.

Ninety percent of Michelangelo's time on the Sistine Chapel ceiling was spent doing the primer.

As a follow-up to her landmark study of gorillas, Dian Fossey spent three years living with guys in monkey suits.

According to a poll in *Film Comment* magazine, fans' least-favorite James Bond was Randy Quaid.

NASA has found evidence of water on Mars, as well as trace amounts of Diet Sprite.

This year's Super Bowl was beaten in the ratings by a rerun of *Wife Swap.*

Just to be safe, five percent of Americans bring their passports when traveling to New Mexico.

Wolf Blitzer has a sign on his front lawn that reads "Beware of the Wolf."

Bob Dylan says the one song he wishes he had written is "Kung Fu Fighting."

The White House Christmas Party is held at Denny's.

LATE SHOW FUN FACTS

In 1946, a powerful windstorm blew away Mount Rushmore's four giant hats.

Basketball great Wilt Chamberlain never made a free throw in an NBA game.

Instead of "selling like hotcakes," Iraqis say "selling like braised goat shanks."

Until 1948, "America the Beautiful" had an additional verse about harassing foreigners.

For Christmas, the pope gave all his coworkers a DVD of Artie Lange's *Beer League.*

When Mr. Ed died, he was ground up and fed to his friend Lassie.

Shaquille O'Neal and Ryan O'Neal are first cousins.

In the 1960s, Fidel and Raul Castro often double-dated Eva and Zsa Zsa Gabor.

Researchers at Chrysler are developing sideview mirrors in which objects may be farther than they appear.

One out of five Good Humor men admits to occasionally squatting in the truck's freezer.

Moses wandered the desert for 40 years because he wouldn't ask for directions.... Am I right, ladies?!

Dinosaurs roamed the earth as recently as 1946.

Milton Berle's mother's sister's children knew him as "Cousin Miltie."

Ingmar Bergman directed *Caddyshack*.

By 2025, the average American will be too fat to fit through a revolving door.

"You're not fully clean unless you're Zestfully clean" is an old Arapaho proverb.

The metric system was doomed due to America's love of foot-long hot dogs.

Because there is no word for "boss" in China, crowds at Bruce Springsteen concerts shout, "Supervisor!"

Eighty-three percent of astronomers admit to pointing their telescope at a sorority house.

The average person swallows 8,000 thumbtacks in his or her lifetime.

Foster Brooks spent six months in a facility to treat fake alcoholics.

Linguists have determined it is impossible to sound sexy when ordering a bagel.

Although the female black widow spider eats the male after mating, most of the males say it's totally worth it.

Although God ordered him to put two of each animal on the ark, Noah got a few extra cows because he liked pot roast.

When Osama bin Laden writes "death to America" in text messages, he uses the abbreviation "d2a."

LATE SHOW FUN FACTS

Thomas Edison also changed the first light bulb.

At the Johns Hopkins School of Medicine, there is an actual Dr. Pepper.

In 1959, DC Comics unveiled a superhero named Waffle Man.

If there is life on another planet, a majority of people hope it's an adorable puppy.

One-third of explorers who've visited both the North and South Poles developed bipolar disorder.

Wesley Snipes withheld millions of dollars in state income tax for years by claiming his primary residence was in New Jack City.

Strict vegetarians will not play Go Fish.

In Nevada, it's illegal for non-magicians to say, "Ta da!"

The ability to walk on water made it difficult for Jesus to swim.

The actor who has won the most Academy Awards is Gary Busey.

In 1972, the World's Fastest Man and the World's Oldest Man were the same person.

The first remote control took eight minutes to change channels.

Wyoming was the first state to allow nude voting.

LATE SHOW FUN FACTS

Completely extended, a standard Slinky can circle the earth three times.

Due to a scheduling mix-up, Jerry Lewis once had to close his show in Vegas by singing "Great Balls of Fire."

In addition to X–ray vision, Superman could also guess your weight within five pounds.

Each year, Hawaii moves four feet closer to Japan.

Each member of the Australian band Men at Work is currently unemployed.

The Dalai Lama has a cousin named Wally Lama.

The 56 original signers of the Declaration of Independence all received complimentary tote bags.

Albert Einstein died before he could prove that one is the loneliest number that you'll ever do.

The New Testament was originally titled *The Old Testament 2.*

At any given moment, 93 percent of American TiVos contain at least one episode of *Sanford & Son.*

Thirty percent of women who apply makeup while driving have accidentally swallowed a tube of lipstick.

At the Vatican, Wednesday night is "spaghetti night."

LATE SHOW FUN FACTS

Before shooting Abraham Lincoln at Ford's Theatre, John Wilkes Booth shot another audience member for making too much noise unwrapping a piece of candy.

According to the Twelfth Amendment to the Constitution, the vice president is entitled to eat any food the president doesn't finish.

At the beginning of his career, Harry Houdini's signature stunt was getting out of dinner with the in-laws.

Whenever Thomas Edison got a woman back to the lab, the light bulbs suspiciously never seemed to work.

Despite using seltzer bottles, clowns often become dehydrated.

Edward R. Murrow's middle name was Rhonda.

One out of every 200 sheep is allergic to wool.

J. Edgar Hoover's last act as director of the FBI was writing the warning that appears at the start of movies.

The FCC's largest indecency fine was given to Lassie for humping an ottoman.

Gerald Ford's Secret Service code name was "Dingus."

REJECTED BY THE FBM!

← Do people still <u>know</u> this show???

Fantasy Island was technically an isthmus.

Before he went into the restaurant business, Colonel Sanders spent free time killing chickens for fun.

(Please run this by legal)

Buddy Ebsen was buried at the Los Angeles dump.

Which L.A. dump? Research, people!!!

Captain Kangaroo's Bob Keeshan died in prison.

No Fun Facts about Keeshan — Friend of Gary Sherman

In Venice, venetian blinds are simply called "blinds."

It's summer, no one's reading. Let's take more chances

Hat sales plummeted when John F. Kennedy became the first president not to regularly wear a hat. Similarly, pants sales plummeted during the Clinton administration.

Gary won't read all this

Three days after making his famous Checkers speech, Richard Nixon had the dog destroyed.

Too much Nixon lately!

Come up with things we'd do if we hadn't already done Nixon

Ninety-three percent of office memos are a waste of time.

What is this, a Dilbert cartoon?

REJECTED BY THE FBMI

Dick Van Dyke has spent ~~the past 40 years~~ *decades* in therapy *seems tepid* trying to get over his fear of white bread.

To make up for a miscalculation by calendar experts, next February will have 40 days. *Not plausible*

Sixty-one percent of Americans say "Coleman" when asked to name their favorite "Dabney." *Already have too many 61% Fun Facts*

Seems kind of high. Double check with Tim in Barber Facts
Twenty-three percent of barbers have unknowingly performed haircuts in their sleep.

Each year more people are killed in Civil War reenactments than were killed in the war itself.

Save it for PBS, Einstein

Shakespeare coined dozens of words including "shopasaurus" and "bridezilla."

What is this? Mad Magazine?!

Reese Witherspoon is ironically allergic to both peanut butter and chocolate.

Note: Reese Witherspoon donates to the FBMI

Once every three years, Mars comes within a mile and a half of Earth.

Nice Try, Asshole

Before the National Association of Realtors decided to simplify, the four rules of real estate were location, location, location, and location.

Archaeologists have found evidence that as far back as the Stone Age, mankind had developed a primitive Swiffer.

During a banana shortage in the summer of 1958, banana splits were made with zucchini.

Beyoncé is so hot, her normal body temperature is 98.7.

Lawrence Welk was a person of interest in several unsolved Hollywood homicides.

In 1951, *Time* magazine's Man of the Year was Moe.

Aristotle is thought to be the first to use the phrase "Having a bad case of the Mondays."

In 1923, meteorologists were baffled when March came in like a lion and went out like a porcupine.

The longest human pregnancy on record was 47 months.

Due to cost-cutting measures, Silly Putty is 23 percent less silly than it used to be.

The most frequently spoken word in the English language is "biscuit."

Nutmeg is 98 percent nut, two percent meg.

The only piece of electrical equipment the Amish are permitted to use is a panini press.

At any given moment, 60 percent of Americans are itchy.

Not until the year 2027 will North Americans witness a total eclipse of the heart.

Pac-Man's ravenous appetite was the result of an enzyme disorder.

The current combined weight of Ben and Jerry is 723 pounds.

In 1994, the NBC *Nightly News* was the first network news show to add a laugh track.

In addition to global warming, Al Gore is warning of an onion ring shortage.

The shish kebab was invented when a Turkish mathematician tried to make an abacus out of meat.

Zachary Taylor, our twelfth president, got his nickname "Old Rough and Ready" from a French whore.

General Tso was allergic to chicken.

Bruce Springsteen's *Born in the USA* album featured a warning to fans to be careful when dancing in the dark.

The largest rat ever killed by a New York City exterminator measured five feet without the tail.

LATE SHOW FUN FACTS

For a brief time, the Bonanno crime family offered summer internships for college credit.

If you say, "Have a nice day" to someone after 5 P.M., it refers to the next day.

Since 1988, a Frisbee has been stuck on the top of the Washington Monument.

Scientists predict that in late 2011, the show *MythBusters* will run out of myths.

In the 1950s, Philip Morris spent millions of dollars trying to teach dogs to smoke.

Before the invention of the ice cream sandwich, people ate frozen BLTs.

The cheetah holds the title of "fastest land animal" and in 1983 also won "most improved."

Nine out of ten visits to Delaware are the result of a wrong turn.

Many historians believe the *Mona Lisa* is smiling because Leonardo da Vinci was telling the model "Yo mama's so fat" jokes.

Dial-A-Mattress cannot guarantee you the best price unless you leave off the last "s" for savings.

During the early '70s, McDonald's briefly offered customers a choice of french fries or consommé.

LATE SHOW FUN FACTS

The most frequently asked question of Americans traveling in foreign countries is, "Do you own an electric skillet?"

The Marlon Brando role in *The Godfather* was originally offered to Andy Griffith.

Sweater-vests came about in the 1920s during a severe sleeve shortage.

After years of research, baseball historians have concluded that no major league team has ever had a first baseman named Who.

The most downloaded song on iTunes is "Wildfire" by Michael Martin Murphey.

Until 1958, people dreamed in black-and-white.

According to the United States Treasury, there are four 15-dollar bills in circulation.

Sixty-five percent of car accidents occur within five miles of an Arby's.

J. Edgar Hoover once wiretapped himself to find out if he was gay.

After administering anesthesia, 70 percent of dentists admit to putting party hats on patients.

The molecular composition of a rain slicker is nearly identical to that of Velveeta.

When making an arrest, the San Diego police have to read a suspect his rights and the surf report.

Until 1958, the winner of the Nobel Prize for Chemistry was determined by applause.

The 2012 Summer Olympics will be held in Bayonne, New Jersey.

Dwight Eisenhower removed his own tonsils with a Swiss Army knife.

Neil Armstrong says the most thrilling experience of his life was the log flume at Six Flags.

In a pinch, pepper spray can be used as a marinade.

Despite their bickering, friends believe that Donald Trump and Rosie O'Donnell will ultimately end up together.

Some biblical scholars believe that during the summer, Jesus turned water into sangria.

Two of Gladys Knight's Pips are now high-ranking Taliban officials.

In 2005, Don Johnson legally changed his name to Nash Bridges.

In addition to his various Scientology works, L. Ron Hubbard published an anthology of Polish jokes.

Dick Van Dyke and Dick Van Patten have agreed to be judges on a new reality show called *America's Next Top Dick Van.*

Because of global warming, Eskimos now only have 16 words for snow.

To advertise its quick-rising breadsticks, Pillsbury briefly made its Doughboy anatomically correct.

Unlike the CIA and FBI, the makers of Cheese Nips and Cheez-Its constantly exchange information.

The second-most-frequently spoken word in the English language is "geyser."

Ronald Reagan is the only president to have lip-synched the oath of office.

If it weren't for a last-minute change to the script, Gary Coleman's famous catchphrase on *Diff'rent Strokes* would have been "What is this in reference to, Willis?"

With a standard pair of dice, it is mathematically impossible to roll a three, five, or eight.

There are currently some 12,000 cowboy hats in the city of Nashville's Lost & Found.

In addition to radioactivity, new Geiger counters can detect cold cuts that have gone bad.

Out of force of habit, astronaut Buzz Aldrin will still occasionally take a leak in his suit.

Eighty-nine percent of parents who bring their children to a PG movie fail to provide any guidance.

Hollywood analysts predict that by 2012, Will Ferrell will run out of sports about which to make movies.

Until 1947, the winner of the Masters Golf Tournament received a green jacket and matching fez.

Mike Wallace was suspended for two weeks by CBS in 1987 when he asked Margaret Thatcher to take off her top.

Harry Truman would often go on vacation and secretly have his twin brother Larry take his place.

Four out of five obese men have gotten their arm stuck in a vending machine.

During a nine-month strike in 2002, the Weather Channel broadcast reruns.

Astrology is a load of horseshit.

Wherever he traveled, Johnny Appleseed planted apple trees and knocked up local women.

Frank Sinatra didn't want to record the song "My Way," but was forced to by his record label.

In China, John Steinbeck's *The Grapes of Wrath* is translated as *Angry Berries.*

Three out of four men feel vaguely uncomfortable eating bananas in public.

David Brenner's master's thesis was entitled "Why Don't They Make the Entire Plane Out of the Black Box?"

Mr. T's name is short for "Tannenbaum."

FBMI SLOGANS

According to the Fourteenth Amendment to the Constitution, every federal agency must have a snappy slogan. Over the years the FBMI's numerous slogans have memorably summed up the FBMI's mission while keeping hundreds of slogan-writers profitably employed.

1891 The FBMI—Purveyor of Diverting Reality-Based Observations Calculated to Arouse the Admiration of Ladies and Gentlemen

1918 The FBMI—Fighting The Hun with Facts That Are Fun!

1925 The FBMI— Fun Facts & Bathtub Gin: Perfect Together!

1929

Brother, Can You Spare A Fact? The FBMI

1951

1955 The FBMI—When It Comes to Fun, Get in Line, Losers.

1967 The FBMI—Fun In, Turn On, Fact Out

1972 Fun Facts—like the Farmers' Almanac, but Less Good-Natured

1976 The FBMI—Ten-Four, Good Miscellaneous Information Buddy!

1969

This slogan got us a cease-and-desist order from the producers of Dragnet.

FBMI SLOGANS

The FBMI
Let The
Fun Facts
★Trickle★

1980

1988 The FBMI—We Are Us.

The FBMI
Betcha Can't Read Just One!

1989

1986 The FBMI—We Do More
Miscellaneous Things by
9 A.M. Than Most People
Do All Day.

1987 The FBMI—Cool. Fresh.
Miscellaneous.

1990 The FBMI—
[no slogan due
to budget cuts]

1991 The FBMI—
Finger-Lickin' Fun!

The FBMI
Time to Put
Your Fun
Pants on!

2000

Fun Factz Are Da Bomb!

2002
*This was part of our
ill-conceived attempt
to appeal to a more
"urban" demographic.*

FUN FACTS
The Only Good Thing to
Come from the Great Satan
America Since Shampoo
and Conditioner in One
Easy Application

ALJAZEERA

2004
*This slogan
appeared
only on Al
Jazeera.*

2007 The FBMI –
Go Fact Yourself!

LATE SHOW FUN FACTS

When Pope John Paul II visited Yankee Stadium in 1979, he struck out six Brewers in five innings of work.

Governor Schwarzenegger devotes an hour each Wednesday to helping California residents with jars they can't open.

Osama bin Laden's favorite movie is *Three Men and a Baby.*

In the last ten years, there have been more e-mails about penis enlargement than in the previous ten centuries combined.

An embarrassed David Blaine once had to call AAA when he locked his keys in his car.

During the early 1970s, Tony Roma's survived two separate scandals in which competitors accused the chain of serving donkey ribs.

Abraham Lincoln's publicist threatened to pull him out of the Lincoln-Douglas debates if he had to speak second.

While recovering from intestinal surgery, Chubby Checker wrote a song about his twisted colon.

Newspaper readers consistently choose Blondie as the comic-strip character they'd most like to see naked.

When *Nightline* can't book an interview with a major politician, they often use look-alikes.

A stranger is just a friend you haven't met.

In addition to rental shoes, some bowling alleys offer rental pants.

Coincidentally, like the cartoon cat, former President James Garfield also loved lasagna and hated Mondays.

In 1999, Certs had to pay a 15-million-dollar fine to the FDA for using black-market Retsyn.

During the last season of *T.J. Hooker,* William Shatner protested the show's cancellation by wearing his hairpiece backward.

In 1983, an Ohio family visiting New York stood at a broken "Don't Walk" sign for three days.

Steak house owner Michael Jordan once played professional basketball.

Biblical scholars recently unearthed a heretofore unknown gospel written by a disciple named Rusty.

During a light caseload season in 1961, the Supreme Court judged beauty contests.

Near Nevada's Area 51 is an area called Area 31, where Baskin-Robbins tests ice cream flavors.

Fabric softener doesn't do anything.

LATE SHOW FUN FACTS

Seventy-five percent of the *Mona Lisa*'s value comes from its frame.

A.1. Steak Sauce was named that so the company would be listed first in the phone book.

Redd Foxx donated generously to the American Heart Association to find a cure for fake heart attacks.

The Smithsonian threw out an early draft of the Constitution to make room for Fonzie's jacket.

Prior to the discovery of penicillin, laughter was the best medicine.

Because of protests, ABC pulled the *Schoolhouse Rock!* episode about the proper way to gut a deer.

In addition to the letter "Z," Zorro was also very good at slashing the number "2."

In Japan, the restaurant Hooters is known as "Owl Calls."

After intensive study of the Shroud of Turin, many theologians now believe that Jesus may have had muttonchops.

Kim Jong Il first came to the attention of the American public as a contortionist on *The Gong Show*.

In the summer, prosthetic limbs are available in red to simulate sunburn.

LATE SHOW FUN FACTS

The completion of *Star Wars* was delayed several weeks when the actor playing Chewbacca dropped gum in his fur.

The book of Leviticus contains a recipe for broccoli polenta.

The Food and Drug Administration is still not sure what to make of bologna.

Since 2002, comedian Jimmie Walker has been strip-searched over 200 times by airport security looking for dy-no-mite.

In 2003, the Recording Industry Association of America came very close to arresting Osama bin Laden for illegal music downloading.

The first laser eye surgery hurt like a son of a bitch.

The building on the back of the 10-dollar bill is Elvis Presley's home, Graceland.

Pope Benedict XVI has declared Mr. Clean Magic Eraser "the work of the devil."

In 1961, NASA studied the viability of having Jackie Gleason punch astronauts to the moon.

To liven up their portraits, courtroom sketch artists often ask witnesses if they have any hobbies.

Herb Peterson, the inventor of the Egg McMuffin, died choking on an Eggo waffle.

Television's first gay kiss featured Ricky Ricardo and Fred Mertz.

The air from the subway grate that blew Marilyn Monroe's skirt up in *The Seven Year Itch* also blew off a cameraman's hairpiece.

Phil Donahue is under the impression that his show has been on hiatus waiting for new carpeting.

Delaware is the only state whose lemon law only applies to actual lemons.

The two most popular baby names in the twelfth century were Genghis and Keith.

An X-treme Gulp at 7-Eleven holds nine gallons of soda.

Thirty-five percent of religions that believe in reincarnation also believe frequent-flyer miles can be used in the next life.

Our shortest president was James Madison at three feet eleven inches.

Intelligence officials now believe that Fidel Castro is faking illness to get sympathy.

LATE SHOW FUN FACTS

When she died, speed-reading pioneer Evelyn Wood was working on a way to watch television more quickly.

Al Gore originally got involved in environmentalism to meet groovy hippie chicks.

Most Americans are uncomfortable chatting about their reproductive organs.

For the last ten years, Henry Kissinger has worked for college art classes as a nude model.

Helen Thomas has slept with the last five presidents.

Much as the plural of "medium" is "media," etymologists say the correct plural of "Steak-umm" is "Steak-a."

Steven Spielberg, David Geffen, and Jeffrey Katzenberg founded DreamWorks to launder money for the Latin Kings.

Because he forgot his boots, Buzz Aldrin walked barefoot on the moon.

By the year 2012, thanks to genetic engineering, we will be enjoying actual buffalo wings.

Although hair does not continue to grow after death, it does become more bouncy and manageable.

Thomas Mann wrote *Death in Venice* after being murdered while visiting Italy.

The Supreme Court was increased from seven justices to nine in 1873 to get into a slo-pitch softball league.

James K. Polk, our eleventh president, did not speak English.

Each year, some 4,000 Americans die installing weather vanes.

It took nearly three years of decomposition for Elvis's corpse to drop below 300 pounds.

In addition to formulating laws about gravity and motion, Newton also observed that if you leave soup out, a skin will form on it.

On days when he had to do a lot of walking, Jesus would turn water into gel for his sandal inserts.

FBMI MERCHANDISE

If you're looking for the perfect gift for that miscellaneous information fan in your life, the FBMI gift shop and Web site offer plenty of great choices!

FBMI MERCHANDISE

FBMI CLERGY VESTMENTS

Clergy of all denominations will appreciate these official FBMI vestments!

MAMA SHERMAN'S POTATO SALAD

Director Gary Sherman's favorite!

FUN FAX FAX MACHINE

Don't just send a fax—
send a "Fun Fax!"

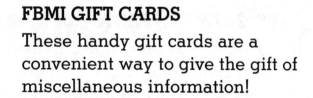

FBMI GIFT CARDS

These handy gift cards are a convenient way to give the gift of miscellaneous information!

FBMI MERCHANDISE

FBMI BABY ONESIES

This handsome onesie gets Baby interested in miscellaneous information early!

LATE SHOW FUN FACTS AUDIO BOOK

Read by Patrick Stewart, the audio version of this book is perfect for guys and gals on the go!

FBMI VITAMINS

Fun Facts Children's Vitamins are tasty, chewable, and info-tricious!

FBMI VITAMINS

EVERY YEAR, 2,300 PEOPLE DIE FROM HORSEPLAY

FBMI-O's

FBMI-O's is a nutritious breakfast cereal for the whole family! Shaped like the letters F, B, M, and I!

LATE SHOW FUN FACTS

Despite the common advertising claim, few gifts that are perfect for dads are also perfect for grads.

When contacted during a 1978 séance, Franklin D. Roosevelt said that he didn't care for his likeness on the dime.

In the Adirondack Mountains, Adirondack chairs are called "chairs."

In Utah, it's illegal to go to T.G.I. Friday's on a Sunday.

Ted Williams's last words were, "I was kidding about being fro..."

In 1998, Michael Jackson paid himself ten million dollars to keep quiet.

The most pointless gossip item Liz Smith ever published was that Randy Quaid has poor penmanship.

Gerald Ford's first job after leaving the White House was providing the voice of Carlton the Doorman on *Rhoda.*

Lemonade and iced tea is called an "Arnold Palmer." Vodka, rum, tequila, and rubbing alcohol is called a "John Daly."

President Bush schooled himself on the ways of war by watching *F Troop.*

Albert Einstein's tremendous intelligence was mostly street smarts.

The FDA has 25 staffers assigned exclusively to gravy.

The Gorton's Fisherman was once sued for asking Mrs. Paul to give him a hand with his dinghy.

Warning: These Fun Facts may contain peanuts.

Due to a calendar mix-up, two years in a row were identified as "1973."

Twenty percent of people who have their appendix removed later decide to have it reinstalled.

In the early drafts of *Moby-Dick,* Moby Dick was a turtle.

In 1997, the Supreme Court ruled that women could be admitted to the Hair Club for Men.

CNN's Lou Dobbs asks his closest friends to call him "L-Dob."

Despite his escape skills, Harry Houdini spent 12 years trapped in a bad marriage.

Archaeologists believe the Great Wall of China was built to keep out Mexicans.

Abraham Lincoln was wearing his stovepipe hat when he lost his virginity.

Since 1917, the Pulitzer Prize committee has given away nearly 2,000 medals, more than 20 million dollars, and two dozen Jet Skis.

LATE SHOW FUN FACTS

More than 30 percent of the world's salt is used to garnish margaritas.

In the four years he was vice president, Dan Quayle used up only one "From the Desk of Dan Quayle" notepad.

Approximately 200,000 drivers a year are seriously burned by E-ZPass sensors.

The United States postmaster general must be able to lick at least 40 stamps per minute.

Every Tuesday is Sloppy Joe Night at the White House.

The most common surname in America is Lipschitz.

The highest-grossing movie of all time is *Crocodile Dundee II.*

Wolf Blitzer got his start as an MTV veejay.

In the world of musicians, no one gets laid like trombone players.

Barbara Walters was once arrested for playing golf naked.

Criminals can elude law-enforcement jurisdiction by fleeing to the International House of Pancakes.

The first item ever patented at the United States Patent and Trademark Office was the patent application form.

LATE SHOW FUN FACTS

Until 1961, popes made their living mostly on tips.

In some parts of Wyoming, it's legal to hunt the elderly.

The Mexican jumping bean has been surpassed in popularity by the smaller, more efficient Japanese jumping bean.

By 2012, Pizza Hut hopes to focus less on pizza sales and more on its hut business.

After breaking his promise not to raise taxes, George H. W. Bush used some of the money to buy a Donkey Kong machine for the White House.

The first baseball caps were made of aluminum.

Lou Ferrigno complains that years after *The Incredible Hulk* went off the air, he'd still turn green when angered.

Each year, 48 customers are accidentally electrocuted at Circuit City.

Yellow Hi-Liter is an excellent source of vitamin C.

Just as Larry is short for Lawrence, Gary is short for Gawrence.

The largest mall in the country, the Mall of America, has 18 Gap stores.

In 1972, in an ill-fated business deal, Amtrak spent four billion dollars to merge with Grand Funk Railroad.

The Incas were the first to develop a system of communication involving foot tapping in men's room stalls.

Wheel of Fortune has been rerunning the same 12 episodes since 1998.

In Los Angeles, there are more breast implants than people.

China's revered General Tso was known to batter-fry his enemies in a tangy orange sauce.

Three out of ten doctors admit to licking the tongue depressors before using them.

Gerald Ford is the only United States president to have walked on the moon.

The average person burns 19 calories giving someone the finger.

Moses's close friends and family members called him "Mo."

Lenny Kravitz has two brothers, Benny Kravitz and Kenny Kravitz.

The most influential invention in history: the printing press.

The least influential invention in history: the tasseled loafer.

To create a nurturing, nonjudgmental atmosphere, many math teachers now tell children that no numbers are truly negative.

LATE SHOW FUN FACTS

Shortly before the end of his life, Elvis Presley was planning to do a film called *Viva Pie.*

The Manhattan Project was followed by the New England project, which was similar but used a thicker, cream-based chowder.

In 1983, the Major League Baseball All-Star Game was played without a ball.

The average vending machine candy bar is four and a half years old.

Because of cigarette burns in the carpet, Dwight Eisenhower didn't get his White House security deposit back.

A 150-pound person weighs 165 pounds in Canada.

The only cabin ever constructed of Duraflame logs burned down in 1988.

A frozen lobster can come back to life when thawed.

In China, Campbell's Alphabet Soup contains more than 3,000 characters.

To save money on alimony, Larry King once married and divorced himself.

The Dalai Lama's birth name was Doug Reynolds Junior.

Albert Einstein's second-favorite theory was "mashed potatoes plus gravy equals delicious."

Many veterinarians in California now offer udder-enhancement surgery.

Only three percent of American homes are equipped with a telegraph.

Due to a misprint, some Gideon's Bibles list "The Gospel According to Mark" as "The Gospel According to Marv."

When it was first introduced, the Butterfinger candy bar was a chocolate-coated stick of butter.

The male cheetah is the fastest animal on Earth, much to the disappointment of the female cheetah.

The human body's largest organ is its skin, except in the case of Milton Berle.

Every United States president with a
beard has been a Republican.

Until 1955, traffic signals also included a
purple light, which meant "up to you."

Ruth Bader Ginsburg often calls Judge
Judy for tips on how to be more sassy in
the courtroom.

In Pakistan, the third Tuesday in January
is "Take Your Mullah to Work Day."

Until last year, National Hockey League games that ended in
a tie were settled by the vice president.

Levi Strauss & Co. lost millions when they marketed a line of
blue jeans for horses.

LATE SHOW FUN FACTS

At five feet nine point two inches, Tim Felder of Provo, Utah, holds the Guinness World Record for the most average height.

Because of his name, Alexander the Great believed he'd grow up to be a magician.

Though Amelia Earhart was never found, her luggage arrived right on time at LaGuardia.

The U.S. Army Corps of Engineers has spent millions of dollars trying to cross a bridge before they come to it.

At the height of *Star Wars* mania, Jimmy Carter gave an Oval Office address in a Chewbacca costume.

Within seven seconds of meeting a man, women subconsciously judge whether they'll ever sleep with him. That time is reduced to less than a second if he's wearing a sweater-vest.

You are more likely to be charged by a rhino than to be pulled over for not wearing your seat belt.

In 1909, Robert Peary became the first explorer to take a leak at the North Pole.

When a movie opens in selected cities, the cities are selected by Burt Reynolds.

The original plans for the Statue of Liberty called for the statue to wave, but France did not want to spend the money.

In order to become licensed, a courtroom sketch artist must demonstrate the ability to make defendants look "shifty."

CAREERS AT THE FBMI

Interested in a career in miscellaneous information? The FBMI is always looking for hardworking, motivated individuals to fill the following positions:

Switchboard Operator. Must be able to effectively manage up to a dozen telephone inquiries per week.

Associate Director, Moscow Bureau. Primary responsibility: Act as a liaison between the FBMI and the KGBMI.

Gary Sherman Look-Alike. Stand in for the FBMI director at public events if he is ill or otherwise engaged.

Driver. Drive the "Fun Facts Mobile," which delivers Fun Facts to schools, street festivals, and the elderly. Valid driver's license required.

CAREERS AT THE FBMI

Proofreader. Check all Fun Facts for spelling and grammer mitakes. Candidate must be 5-3 years experience.

Nighttime Receptionist. Answer phones for night-shift FBMI staff. Transfer emergency calls to Gary Sherman's home(s) as necessary. Receptionist is not authorized to dispense Fun Facts over the phone!

Associate Director, Fun Facts International. Assemble team for the FBMI's planned Mexico branch; coordinate 2010 launch of "Hechos Agradables." Spanish a plus, but not necessary.

Warehouse Foreman. Manage the intake, storage, and distribution of Fun Facts at the FBMI's local facility in Bethesda, Maryland.

Responsible for maintaining ideal conditions for Fun Fact storage: 64 degrees Fahrenheit and humidity of 48 percent.

Claims Examiner. Responsible for reviewing claims submitted by people professing to have been injured by unsettling Fun Facts.

More information and applications available at fbmi.gov. The Federal Bureau of Miscellaneous Information is an Equal Opportunity Employer, and does not discriminate on the basis of age, sex, race, religion, color, national origin, sexual orientation, disability, marital status, weight, height, ridiculous hair, intelligence, or talent.

FBMI JOB APPLICATION

Answer all questions completely and truthfully. All information will be verified by FBMI researchers.

Last name_____ First name_____

Middle initial _____Second letter of middle name _____

Address_____

City_____State _____ Zip + 4: _____Zip + 4 + 5 (if known):_____

❑ *Check here if the Google Maps satellite image of this address shows someone sunbathing on the roof.*

Phone _____Cell _____

Did you actually pay $600 for an iPhone? ___ yes   ___ no

Date of birth _____

Celebrities who share your birthday _____

E-mail _____

❑ *Check here if you would like to receive e-mail about discount prescription drugs, mortgage refinancing, or virility enhancement products*

Are you a U.S. citizen? __ yes   __ Draj kvóznyrgzni, zo lùzqfiljo, USA, USA!

List any jobs previously held with a U.S. government agency. If you were an undercover CIA agent, put "Office Supply Procurement." If you actually procured office supplies for the U.S. government, put "Classified."

_____

_____

If you worked for the General Services Administration, please explain what the General Services Administration is:

_____

_____

List any embarrassing personal information (i.e., "dirt") you happen to know about employees of other federal agencies, especially the Bureau of Weights & Measures:

_____

_____

What position are you applying for at the FBMI? _____

Hobbies? _____

Pets?_____ Pets' hobbies? _____

The FBMI is always looking to improve its softball team. List any baseball/softball strengths you may have, and indicate what equipment you own:

_____

_____

Optional: Are you on the Juice? __ yes __ no __ not knowingly

List any ideas for sabotaging the softball team from the Bureau of Weights & Measures:

_____

_____

❑ *Check here to indicate "I have read and understood the FBMI's official policy on office relationships between young female employees and Director Gary Sherman" (policy available for review at fbmi.gov).*

By my signature below, I attest that I have answered all questions truthfully and accurately to the best of my knowledge. I solemnly swear that I am not a mole from the Bureau of Weights & Measures. I agree that, in addition to using the information contained herein for judging my suitability for employment, the FBMI may publish the information in the form of potentially embarrassing Fun Facts.

Signature _____ Date _____

Submit this application, along with your résumé, three references, and a voluntary contribution to the FBMI Benevolent Association to FBMI, Personnel Department, Box 23000002, Washington, DC 20432.

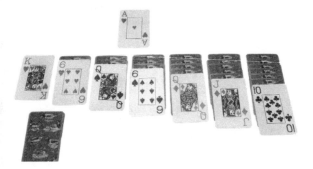

The lowest-rated cable program ever was ESPN2's coverage of the World Series of Solitaire.

Bill Clinton is the only president to have received a lap dance at his inauguration.

The National Weather Service has three employees who do nothing but watch for clouds that look like animals.

According to conspiracy theorists, there is significant evidence that *Cheers* was not filmed before a live studio audience.

During the great powdered cheese shortage of 1965, schoolchildren ate macaroni and hummus.

After nursing, Florence Nightingale's second love was keno.

The 1983 New York City Marathon took three days to complete when runners were required to pay a toll before crossing the Verrazano-Narrows Bridge.

When asked about his hair, Donald Trump once admitted that as a teenager he was bitten by a radioactive muskrat.

Instead of "too much junk in the trunk," the British say "too much fruit in the boot."

LATE SHOW FUN FACTS

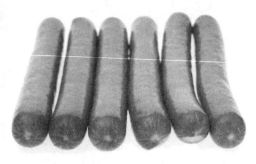

In accordance with Old Testament law, every Hebrew National hot dog is circumcised.

In Tutankhamen's tomb, a stone jar marked "nuts" proved to contain a single-function, spring-loaded snake.

Three out of ten paramedics admit they lost their virginity to a CPR dummy.

In 2003, Queen Elizabeth II replaced her throne with Archie Bunker's chair.

Arnold Schwarzenegger has handpicked Lou Ferrigno to replace him as governor of California in 2010.

President Hoover is buried in the Hoover Dam.

Drew Carey got the *Price Is Right* job after correctly guessing what his salary would be without going over.

At least twice a day, someone sarcastically refers to David Blaine as "Siegfried."

While doing some shadowboxing, Mike Tyson once bit off his own shadow's ear.

In 1961, engineers at IBM developed the prototype of the Miami Sound Machine.

Fifteen percent of Americans don't care for the remaining 85 percent of Americans.

In foreign markets, the hit CBS show *CSI* is titled *Carpet Fiber Squad.*

LATE SHOW FUN FACTS

Jacques Cousteau died attempting to plug a lamp into an electric eel.

When William the Conqueror was in high school, he was voted "Most Likely to Conquer Something."

The Dallas/Fort Worth International Airport is larger than New York City's Manhattan Island.

In 1986, Kraft briefly sold a complement to Cheez Whiz called Meat Whiz.

Although not unheard of, knock-knock jokes were relatively rare before the invention of the door.

At least once a week, Tommy Lee Jones receives a piece of mail addressed to David Lee Roth.

In 1964, the world's tallest man lost his title after getting a haircut.

By 2010, mathematicians hope to replace long division with wide division.

When Donald Trump travels to the Southern Hemisphere, his comb-over automatically changes from counterclockwise to clockwise.

The correct response to the Irish greeting "Top o' the morning to you" is "Rot in hell, suckbag."

Although Albert Einstein's brain was preserved after his death, it was accidentally thrown away when Mrs. Einstein cleaned out her pantry.

LATE SHOW FUN FACTS

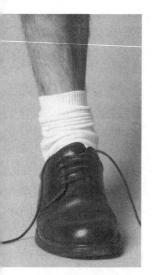

Telling someone their shoelace is untied is the least appreciated act of kindness.

Chinese restaurants require Peking duck to be ordered 24 hours in advance so the duck may enjoy one last day with its family.

Colonel Sanders received a dishonorable discharge from the army for refusing to divulge his 11 secret herbs and spices.

In 2008, Downy is planning to introduce a line of scented fabric hardeners.

The Civil War was fought over whether to call it the "Mason-Dixon Line" or the "Dixon-Mason Line."

A broken digital clock is right zero times a day.

Seventy-five percent of the Earth is covered by water. Fifteen percent is covered by linoleum.

A person is considered "highfalutin" if their falutin count is over 170.

Harlem Globetrotter Curly Neal holds the record for most fake assists.

The average Canadian consumes half a gallon of maple syrup daily.

Guinness holds the world record for the largest collection of records.

Don't let the birthday greetings fool you; Willard Scott hates the elderly.

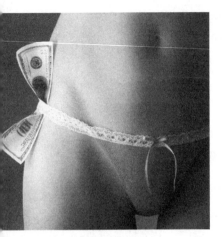

Exotic dancers have been lobbying the government to make currency out of a softer, less abrasive paper.

The Subway restaurant chain has stockpiled more than 50 commercials featuring Jared just in case he gets fat again.

In early drafts of *Star Wars,* Darth Vader and Luke Skywalker are fraternity brothers who go to Tijuana for spring break.

Due to a clerical error, until 1951, Virginia's state motto was "Virginia is for losers."

Close examination of the dime reveals that Roosevelt is sweaty.

Ninety people a year die due to accidents involving three-hole punches.

Buzz Aldrin is the only man to have lost his virginity in space.

In 1977, jackhammer-wielding vandals altered Mount Rushmore to make Washington look like Mickey Rooney.

For the first few years of his career, Barack Obama went by the name of Barack Cougar Obamacamp.

In the final episode of *The Honeymooners,* the Kramdens and Nortons died from a gas leak in their building.

Hardware stores in Utah require male and female pipe couplings to be kept in separate aisles.

LATE SHOW FUN FACTS

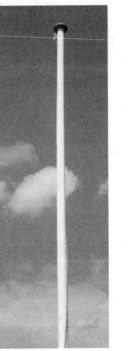

Flagstaff, Arizona is the largest United States city named for a kind of pole.

Babe Ruth's last words were, "The money's on the dresser."

Milton Bradley invented the game Twister as an excuse to touch women at parties.

Ironically, 200 Americans a year die of choking on Life Savers.

Mitt Romney has paid thousands of dollars to a blackmailer who has photos of him with his tie askew.

To ensure prompt delivery of e-mail, the post office recommends affixing a 42-cent stamp to your computer.

Bald men die two percent financially better-off thanks to savings on haircuts.

In the 1970s, NASA spent two billion dollars to convert the Jefferson Airplane into the Jefferson Starship.

In his later years, King Kong was mostly limited to climbing ranch houses.

Before performing each miracle, Jesus yelled, "Shazam!"

Franklin Roosevelt wasn't sick, he just used the wheelchair as an excuse to get out of sex with Eleanor.

After accidentally washing his wardrobe in hot water, Johnny Cash was briefly known as "The Man in Gray."

LATE SHOW FUN FACTS

Aside from man, the raccoon is the only animal that flosses.

Though a man of peace, don't even try to talk to the Dalai Lama before his morning coffee.

Before television became common-place, a young Elvis Presley entertained himself by shooting his radio.

The first known mention of a food being "finger-lickin' good" is in the book of Leviticus.

In addition to "The buck stops here," Harry Truman had another sign on his desk that read, "No fat chicks."

Arnold Schwarzenegger was 23 years old before he could spell his last name.

The smallest bunch of bananas ever recorded: one banana.

PHOTO CREDITS